D1740508

Crucified with Christ

Crucified with Christ

Meditation on the Passion, Mystical Death,
and the Medieval Invention
of Psychotherapy

Dan Merkur

State University of New York Press

Published by
State University of New York Press, Albany

© 2007 State University of New York

All rights reserved

Printed in the United States of America

No part of this book may be used or reproduced in any manner whatsoever
without written permission. No part of this book may be stored in a retrieval system
or transmitted in any form or by any means including electronic, electrostatic,
magnetic tape, mechanical, photocopying, recording, or otherwise
without the prior permission in writing of the publisher.

For information, address State University of New York Press,
194 Washington Avenue, Suite 305, Albany, NY 12210-2384

Production by Michael Haggett
Marketing by Anne M. Valentine

Library of Congress Cataloging-in-Publication Data

Merkur, Daniel
    Crucified with Christ : meditation on the passion, mystical death, and the medieval
invention of psychotherapy / Dan Merkur.
        p. cm.
    Includes bibliographical references and index.
    ISBN-13: 978-0-7914-7105-0 (hardcover : alk. paper)
    ISBN-13: 978-0-7914-7106-7 (pbk. : alk. paper)
1. Jesus Christ—Crucifixion. 2. Psychoanalysis and religion. 3. Catholic Church and psychoanalysis. 4. Psychotherapy. I. Title.
    BT453.M47   2007
    261.5'15—dc22

2006020828

10 9 8 7 6 5 4 3 2 1

maninder bains

Contents

Preface

In this book, I argue that Western psychotherapy was invented through a con-
fluence of several factors in the twelfth through fourteenth centuries. Cistercian monks and, later, Franciscan friars and other Christian contemplatives
developed a form of meditation on the passion of Jesus that produced personality change with sufficient regularity to attract the attention of spiritual directors such as James of Milan, whose *Stimulus amoris*, "Goad of Love," will be
discussed in chapter 1.

In *The Ladder of Perfection*, Walter Hilton, an English Augustinian canon
of the late fourteenth century, went further. He claimed that with the grace of
God, "reformation of faith and feeling" was a predictable or a reliable effect of
meditation; and he published detailed descriptions of its vicissitudes. In chapter 2, I review his claims and establish that wholesome personality change,
consistent with psychoanalytic standards for the evaluation of personality
change, was indeed what he was describing.

Granting that meditation on the passion achieved personality change, how
did it do so? Both St. Bonaventure and the Blessed Heinrich Süse (Henry Suso)
remarked that they knew two approaches to the meditation. In one technique,
the meditator adopted the perspective of an eyewitness of the crucifixion,
empathizing with St. Mary, St. John, or another who attended Jesus on the cross.
In chapter 3, I explain why I think this practice was sometimes psychohygienic
or sometimes pathogenic, but not systematically psychotherapeutic.

In the other meditative technique, which I discuss in chapter 4, the meditator adopted the perspective of Jesus, underwent crucifixion with Christ, and
so personally experienced and not merely witnessed death and resurrection.
Because Milan and Hilton both referred exclusively to the second approach,
we may infer that experiences of mystical death were a decisive aspect of the
therapeutic action of the meditations.

In chapter 5, I offer a psychoanalytic interpretation of the therapeutic
action of crucifixion with Christ. So far as possible, my hypothesis keeps to the
medieval evidence, which I conceptualize from a psychoanalytic perspective.
My interpretation draws primarily on the object relations theories of Melanie

Klein, D. W. Winnicott, and Neville Symington. These several psychoanalytic perspectives have been synthesized, with as little jargon as possible, with the revised model of the superego that I proposed in *Unconscious Wisdom* (Merkur, 2001).

Having established (to my thought conclusively) that Hilton's technique of meditation was consistent with the evidence of personality change that he documented, I turn, in chapter 6, to the paradigm shift in Hilton's understanding of conversion. It is my claim that a theological move within Christianity, exemplified by St. Francis of Assisi, informed a change in religious discourse from talk about the experience of God to talk about conformance with the example of Jesus. Through St. Bonaventure, theology yielded to psychology as an intellectual discipline for thinking about mystical experiences. Voluntary aspects of the experiences, formerly shunned as theurgical, were now conceptualized as unobjectionable processes within the human soul. When, in the fourteenth century, the practical impact of mystical experiences on mystics' lives became the criterion for their assessment, the self-conscious facilitation of personality change became integral to the work of spiritual directors such as Hilton.

For their bibliographic help and comments, I thank Claire Fanger, Joseph Goering, Bernard McGinn, Joanne McWilliams, Nicholas Watson, and Elliot R. Wolfson. I thank Gerald J. Gargiulo and Keith Haartman for reading and commenting on the manuscript. I also want to acknowledge the input of the anonymous readers for SUNY Press, whose comments were extremely helpful. I alone am responsible, of course, for all errors of omission and commission. I thank my children Matthew, Jeremy, Kira, and Isaiah, who share their father with his books, mostly with good grace; and I dedicate this book to my ex, Lara Huntsman, who made the writing possible in so many different ways.

Acknowledgments

The author has made every effort to trace the ownership of all copyrighted material. In the event of any question concerning reprint permissions, the author expresses regret for any error that he may have made and will gladly make the necessary correction in future editions of this book. Thanks are due to the following authors, editors, publishers, and publications for permission to reprint materials from the following publications:

Excerpts from *Bonaventure: The Soul's Journey Into God, The Tree of Life, The Life of St. Francis* from the Classic of Western Spirituality translated and introduced by Ewart Cousins, Copyright © 1978 The Missionary Society of St. Paul the Apostle of the State of New York, Paulist Press, Inc., New York and Mahwah, NJ. Used with permission of Paulist Press. *www.paulistpress.com*

Excerpts from *The Works of Bonaventure: Cardinal, Seraphic Doctor and Saint, Vol. 1: Mystical Opuscula*, translated by Jose de Vinck. Paterson, NJ: St. Anthony Guild Press, 1960. Copyright © 1960 St. Anthony's Guild.

Excerpts from *Dialogues* by Saint Gregory the Great, Fathers of the Church series Vol. 39, translated by Odo John Zimmerman. Copyright © 1959 Catholic University of America Press. Used with permission: The Catholic University of America Press, Washington, DC.

Excerpts from The Ladder of Monks by Guigo II, translated by Edmund colledge and James Walsh, Copyright © 1978 by Edmund Colledge and James Walsh. Used by permission of Doubleday, a division of Random House, Inc.

Excerpts from *Walter Hilton: The Scale of Perfection* from the Classics of Western Spirituality translated and introduced by John P. H. Clark and Rosemary Dorward. Copyright © 1991 John P. H. Clark and Rosemary Dorward, Paulist Press, Inc., New York and Mahwah, NJ. Used with permission of Paulist Press. *www.paulistpress.com*

Excerpts from *Pseudo Dionysius: The Complete Works* from the Classics of Western Spirituality translated by Colm Luibheid, foreword, notes, and translation collaboration by Paul Rorem. Copyright © 1978 Colm Luibheid, Paulist Press, Inc., New York and Mahwah, NJ. Used with permission of Paulist Press. *www.paulistpress.com*

Excerpts from *Henry Suso: the Exemplar, with Two German Sermons* from the Classics of Western Spirituality translated by Frank Tobin. Copyright © 1989 Frank Tobin, Paulist Press, Inc., New York and Mahwah, NJ. Used with permission of Paulist Press. *www.paulistpress.com*

Chapter 1

Turned Without and Within

A small body of recent psychoanalytic findings indicates that when mystical experiences produce personality changes, they do so in the same manners as psychoanalysis. Most mystical experiences do not meet psychoanalytic standards of therapeutic success; but cross-cultural examples that meet psychoanalytic criteria have been documented in Navajo healing and Inuit shamanism (Merkur, 2005), the biblical tales of Abram and Job (Merkur, 1995–96, 2004), the conversion of St. Ignatius Loyola (Meissner, 1999), the conversions produced through John Wesley's method in eighteenth century British Methodism (Haartman, 2004), possibly the story of Arjuna's encounter with Shiva in the Hindu Bhagavad Gita (Reddy, 2001), and possibly also in the narratives of Milarepa and Naropa in the Kagyu lineage of Tibetan Buddhism (Finn, 1998, 2003). Whether mystical or psychoanalytic, wholesome personality change evidently depends on common processes of therapeutic action.

These findings suggest that therapeutic personality change mobilizes a naturally occurring healing process that has historically been conceptualized in a variety of religious and secular manners. Freud (1933) was evidently of a similar opinion:

> It is easy to imagine . . . that certain mystical practices may succeed in upsetting the normal relations between the different regions of the mind, so that, for instance, perception may be able to grasp happenings in the depths of the ego and in the id which were otherwise inaccessible to it. It may safely be doubted, however, whether this road will lead us to the ultimate truths from which salvation is to be expected. Nevertheless it may be admitted that the therapeutic efforts of psychoanalysis have chosen a similar line of approach. Its intention is, indeed,

1

to strengthen the ego, to make it more independent of the super-ego, to widen its field of perception and enlarge its organization, so that it can appropriate fresh portions of the id. Where id was, there ego shall be. It is a work of culture—not unlike the draining of the Zuider Zee. (pp. 79–80)

Freud denied that metaphysical truth and salvation may be attained through mysticism. However, he acknowledged that psychoanalysis proceeds in a fashion that is similar to mysticism and he implied that mysticism, like psychoanalysis, is properly to be regarded as "a work of culture." It is or can be a means to facilitate psychotherapeutic healing.

The concept of a naturally occurring process of psychological healing has implications for the history of psychotherapy. The natural healing process has been remarked from time immemorial in a variety of different cultures. Several religious traditions devised techniques to facilitate the occurrence of the natural healing process long before equivalent procedures were conceptualized in the manner that led to their designation in 1887 as psychotherapeutics (Pivnicki, 1969). The conceptual shift from a religious paradigm to a naturalistic approach was a comparatively recent achievement. This book concerns a shift in the fourteenth century within Christian mystical theology, when the traditional concern with spiritual access to supernatural beings and locations, was replaced with a concern with the effect of divine grace on processes within the human soul. The metaphysical question: Is this contemplation true? was replaced for pragmatic purposes by the psychological question: Is this contemplation good for you?

James of Milan

To begin my narrative, let us examine the *Stimulus amoris* of James of Milan, a late medieval devotional text that was often mistakenly attributed to St. Bonaventure. James of Milan discussed a technique of meditation that scholars term "meditation on the passion," and he remarked that the fruits of meditation on the passion of Jesus included occasional spontaneous occurrences of the soul's conformity with the sweetness of Jesus. It is my claim that he was discussing what we may today recognize as therapeutic personality change.

James of Milan was a Franciscan of the late thirteenth and early fourteenth centuries who is known to us almost entirely through the one text. The Latin text of the *Stimulus amoris* is extant in two markedly different rescensions (Fleming, 1977). The text was repeatedly augmented with additions that were placed both before and after the original composition by James of Milan. The developed manuscript was translated into Middle English in the late fourteenth century under the title *The Prickynge of Love*. The translation includes notable interpolations by the translator. Three of the ten surviving manuscripts of *The Prickynge of Love*, including one at Cambridge, name the translator as Walter Hilton (Hilton, 1952, p. 19). An English translation of the Latin manuscript was made and published in 1642, before being revised, edited, and published again in 1907 (Bonaventure, 1907). A modern translation of the Middle English translation was published in 1952 (Hilton, 1952). For present purposes, I have quoted Clare Kirchberger's translation of the Middle English version, which identifies the medieval translator's additions with angle << >> brackets.

James of Milan referred to meditation on the passion in summary terms that implied the reader's familiarity with the details of the meditative technique.

> Unless I may have passion and compassion with Christ, as St. Paul saith, I shall not reign with Christ. But what is more fruitful and sweet than for to bear in our hearts full compassion of Christ's passion . . . ? Nothing here in this life! And what is more worthy than to be like God's son Jesus Christ? Soothly nothing. But how may we be like to him in heaven, when we are all unlike to him in our <<life here>>? What is more vlatsome than to see God's son in man, suffer wrongs, shames, reproofs and vilest death, for me a stinking wretch . . . ? (Hilton, 1952, pp. 121–22)

The phrase "to bear in our hearts full compassion of Christ's passion" explained the emotion that was to be cultivated through meditation on the passion. The wording "to see God's son in man, suffer wrongs, shames, reproofs and vilest death" referred to the use of mental imagery by which one might see the events of the passion in one's imagination.

For James of Milan, meditation on the passion was a routine component of preparation to receive the Eucharist. The sacrament of the altar was to be interpreted as a type of the passion:

> And namely then, when he shall go to Mass that he greithe him thus. First that he withdraw his mind from all outward things and gather himself all whole into himself if he may, so entirely that neither he be scattered by bodily wits nor by vain thoughts. And then ransack his own conscience and that that he findeth unclean, that he wash it away with tears of compunction. And go to his confessor and cast out through meek shrift all venom of sin. And when he has done yet eft lift up his heart and think on the meekness of God and of the wretchedness of himself; how much and how worthy God is, how little and how unworthy himself is, and thus nought himself. <<And

thank God>> so that he be as he were turned into God, that he see none other thing nor feel but God. Then, <<if time suffer>>, he may think also of the great love of our Lord, that would to himself, that is so worthy (take) on him the vileness of mankind; and then he may think points of Christ's passion for to stir his own heart to compassion. And over that, for to wonder of his wonderful charity, that not only would offer himself for us on the cross, but he offereth himself to us in sacrament of the altar, for to be fully with us and in us. (pp. 139–40).

After meditation on one's sins and making confession, a person was to "think points of Christ's passion for to stir his own heart to compassion." Identification with Jesus formed a component of the meditation. A meditator was to "be as he were turned into God" before he thought "points of Christ's passion."

James of Milan also regarded meditation on the passion as one of three preparations that a person might make to receive consolation in the form of contemplation of Christ.

The second is that thou strengthen thee in all that thou mayst for to have compassion of Christ's passion, overall bearing it in thy heart, for but if we can have compassion, we may not receive consolation. If thou mayst think on his passion deeply and mayst enter with thine affection into the wound of his side, thou shalt soon then come to his heart and <<then thou mayst rest thee there as in thy bedstead>>. Whoso weeneth to come to contemplation of Christ and cometh not by this door <<nor by this way nor by the bitterness (and compassion) of Christ in his manhood>>, he is but a thief and a micher, for when he weeneth to be within, he is full far without. (pp. 142–43)

The third preparation was to be mindful of the omnipresence of Jesus (p. 143), a traditional topic of Christian contemplation.

The effect of meditation on the passion was a transformation into Christ. The transformation began with the horrors of the passion but led presently to Christ's living embrace.

This is a gracious change, worth much good, for to change the wounds of sin into the wounds of Christ, and filth of his soul into <<Christ's cleanness, (his pride into Christ's meekness)>>, and his vileness into <<Christ's>> majesty, his own malice into <<Christ's>> goodness, his own bitterness into <<Christ's>> sweetness <<and his own darkness into Christ's light. Then might he say with Paul: 'I live and not I for Christ liveth in me.' [Galatians ii, 20] Thus is a man

➡ turned into Christ, that hath spoiled himself of himself and with full
offering of his soul to Christ is clothed and lapped all in the love of
Christ. (p. 145)

A meditator would undergo a gracious change by which his personal wounds
of sin became the wounds of Christ crucified. Later the bitterness would turn
to sweetness.

Turning into Christ in this manner was conceptualized specifically as a
mystical union. In a later passage, James of Milan asserted that a "man . . . may
perfectly be oned to God and changed into him." (p. 146)

James of Milan remarked that meditation on the passion led to two different emotional reactions. "A deep and an inly [=inward] beholding of Christ's
passion" might be followed by a drunkenness that consisted of gladness, mirth,
merriment, and a perception of Christ's presence in all creatures.

> The first drunkenness is a great abundance of gladsomeness and an high
> mirth of heart <<that cometh so suddenly into a soul>> through a new
> lightning <<of Christ's presence>>, after mickle weeping going before or
> after a deep and an inly beholding of Christ's passion; or else after great
> fervour of desire long kindled <<through assidual beholding of Christ.
> These are soothfast chesons and not deceivable>>. And this gladness
> when it is conceived, increaseth so mickle within, that it reboundeth into
> the body and maketh <<all limbs>> for to be fain <<and merry of
> Christ's comforting>>. And sometimes for our mickle gladness they stir
> and may suffer no resting <<in a manner as a man were drunk>>. And
> in this time <<the soul is so stirred through mickleness of Christ's love
> that her thinketh she may find Christ in all creatures>> and liketh for to
> halse them. But the heart is not bowing to vain delight of the creature
> but only <<of Christ in the creature>>. (Hilton, 1952, p. 152)

James of Milan did not refer to "drunkenness" as a contemplative state,
even though his description of the soul thinking that "she may find Christ in
all creatures" corresponds to one of two major topics of Christian contemplation. Monks traditionally aspired to "the contemplation of the physical world,
and . . . the contemplation of God" (Evagrius, 1981, p. 19).

A second reaction that a soul might make to meditation on the passion differed from the first by not translating into physical activity. Neither did it entail
a contemplation of Christ's immanence in all creatures. The impact of meditation remained within the soul and was, for that reason, possibly a deception.

> Another drunkenness is this: when a man in contemplation . . .
> feeleth his heart filled with a wonderful sweetness through Christ's

presence, and this sweetness so mickle aboundeth in the heart that all limbs of the body take part of it, so far forth that a man thinketh all his feeling without or within sweeter than honey. . . . this drunkenhead that is cause of over mickle sweetness maketh the body for to rest in stillness. . . . in this drunkenhead may come deceit. . . . For why?>> the fiend . . . would that a man had pride and set well by himself for feeling of such sweetness and that he fully feed himself in such manner delights as in full rest of his soul, and so by this manner way shall he be turned from God, <<for he would none other beholding have but only feeling of such sweetness. Thus are some contemplatives deceived>>. . . . Some contemplatives <<when they feel aught of God>>, anon they presume of themselves and despise other men and weenen that they are next God, when they are through pride full far cast from him. (Hilton, 1952, p. 152)

What James of Milan described in this passage was a "unitive distortion" (Haartman, 2001) or pathological complication of mystical experience, of the variety that Carl G. Jung (1952, p. 315) termed "inflation." It is a grandiosity over the fact of having had a mystical experience. It substitutes self-importance for religious devotion to God. James of Milan was sufficiently astute to recognize that the grandiosity coincides with contempt for others.

The fiend "casteth . . . in suggestions of pride and of presumption: that a man ween himself: (he) is contemplative and <<great in God's sight>>, and then deemeth he all other vicious and <<defaulty. The least default that ever other men doeth, he seeth it and riseth against it unpatiently. But he seeth right nought or little of himself,>> and taketh upon himself unwisely the authority (of the Apostle). (Hilton, 1952, p. 156; compare p. 162)

And now we come to the particular passages of our keenest concern. James of Milan also noted responses to mystical experience that we may recognize as changes not of moods but of long-term character. He remarked, for example, that differing extents of change were to be expected of novices and past practitioners of meditation.

That devotion which thou travailest after for to have, is in others, had of old, and mightily rooted in them, and that may be a cause why them seem not so stirred by outward tokens about ghostly profit as thou art. For why? ghostly sweetness when it is fresh <<and new felt>> maketh open changing of a man, but I hope it doth not so in him, that hath been through devotion, stirred and changed, of old.

And therefore when thou seest thyself melt all into water for devotion, and other God's servants not so, think then that it is well.
(Hilton, 1952, pp. 162-63)

Because past practitioners had already undergone profound changes, spiritual
experiences no longer transformed them as dramatically.

What sorts of changes took place? The *Stimulus amoris* noted that conformity with Christ sometimes took form as a general sweetening of the personality. "And some also through grace wax ripe, so that they are all turned
<<into Christ's sweetness>> without and within, and all bitterness is cut from
their hearts so cleanly that they seem more woning in heaven than in earth"
(Hilton, 1952, p. 163). James of Milan described what we may understand as
conflict solution that ended bitterness and left them "turned without and
within" in a manner that was more appropriate to heaven than to earth.

In other cases, however, corruption prevailed: "And also some are waxend
as trees and ever profiting in God's grace from day to day. And some <<rot>>
and turn to corruption as wicked men do." (Hilton, 1952, p. 163)

The hope to conform with the pure spirituality of God had led the fourth
century Desert Father Evagrius Ponticus (1981) to advocate *apatheia*, an emotional indifference to the material world, as an ideal for mystics to achieve. The
monastic goal of apatheia was attached to meditation on the passion, for example, in *Christ Crucified*, a fourteenth century text by an anonymous Benedictine
monk of Farne.

The third degree is reached when a man is so fired with the love of
God that he is neither elated by prosperity nor cast down by adversity, and if riches abound, he by no means sets his heart on them; if
he happen to lose them, it causes him no regret at all.
    This is the wisest and most perfect love of God and is itself proof
that all worldly love is dead. (Monk of Farne, 1961, p. 90)

A Friar Minor, James of Milan entertained a significantly different ideal.
Jesus, whose lifestyle Franciscans sought to emulate, had by no means been
indifferent to material creatures. The reaction to meditation that James of
Milan singled out for praise was not an indifference but a powerful emotional
engagement "without and within." Meditators achieved it when "all bitterness
is cut from their hearts." The Middle English translator of *Stimulus amoris*,
who was probably Walter Hilton, added the phrase "into Christ's sweetness."

Beginning with the conversion of St. Paul on the road to Damascus,
Christian reports of transformative mystical experiences discussed the events
as miracles that occurred spontaneously as gifts of grace. James of Milan inno-
vated by discussing personality change as an occasional effect of a particular

type of meditation. We may assume that similar reactions to meditation had been experienced by many individuals over the centuries. However, it was Francis of Assisi's expansion of the Church's ministry from the City of God into the City of Man that made it possible for Christians to conceptualize conformance with Christ's sweetness in a positive manner. The monastic ideal of *apatheia* had depended on a Platonic view of spirit in opposition to matter and the body as a prison for the soul. Franciscan devotion to Christ instead emphasized the theological doctrine of the Incarnation of God, not only in the person of the historical Jesus, but also in the Word's continuing presence throughout creation. To be Christ-like in the world, with a sweetness and an absence of bitterness, was understood as an ideal that was valid in its own right. It was not a failure to attain perfect detachment. Apathetic withdrawal from the world was not the only salvific option.

As a Franciscan, James of Milan welcomed therapeutic personality change. He did not see it as a failure to attain *apatheia*. However, he did not prioritize conformance with Christ as the goal of his meditations. The decisive step from a welcome occurrence to a deliberate procedure was instead taken by Walter Hilton, who was very likely the Middle English translator of *Stimulus amoris* (Clark, 1984). Hilton made the claim in his *Scala perfectionis* that "reforming in faith and feeling" can reliably be cultivated, with God's grace, through meditation on the passion. Centuries earlier than anyone presently dates the invention of psychotherapy (compare Zilboorg & Henry, 1941; Kirschner, 1996), his claim deserves close attention.

Chapter 2

Reforming in Faith and Feeling

Walter Hilton died on March 24, 1396 as a Canon of St. Augustine at Thurgarton Priory, near Southwell in Nottinghamshire, England. The manuscript tradition asserts that he was an Inceptor in Canon Law, having qualified for the doctorate but not having taken the degree. He referred in one letter to his legal background; and there is good evidence that he was educated at Cambridge University, graduating in Civil Law by 1370. His studies at Cambridge must have commenced no later than 1357, making his date of birth likely no later than 1343. By 1375, Hilton was a Bachelor of Civil Law appearing in an ecclesiastical court. His studies in Canon Law would belong to the late 1370s. By the mid 1380s, Hilton had abandoned his academic career and become an anchorite, spending his life as a solitary in contemplation. We possess a letter to Adam Horsley, from around 1384, in which Hilton remarked he was unsure of his vocation. Around 1386, he moved on to become an Augustinian Canon at Thurgarton Priory. This move represented an embrace of community and a commitment to a mixed life that combined the contemplative and active lives. Although some time would have been given over to the pursuit of contemplation, Hilton would have been active as a teacher and spiritual guide. His legal expertise may also have been put to use. In 1388, the Prior at Thurgarton, among others, was authorized to arrest, examine, and imprison heretics; and Hilton may have been involved in legal actions against Lollards, Free Spirits, and others (Clark & Dorward, 1991, pp. 13–16).

Several of Hilton's extant writings reflect his career path. The Middle English text, which an editor named *The Scale of Perfection*, is an editorial combination of two books (Hilton, 1979, pp. 5, 42, 343). The first, addressed to an enclosed anchoress, advocates the contemplative life in explicitly Augustinian terms. It presumably dates to his arrival at Thurgarton Priory. His *Epistle on the Mixed Life* is addressed to a nobleman whom he discouraged from the contemplative life and instead urged him to embrace his station in life (Beale, 1975). The text reflects the change of heart that accompanied Hilton's own mixed life at Thurgarton. Book Two of the *Scale* similarly advocates a mixed life.

As may be expected of an Austin canon, Hilton articulated his mystical theology in Augustinian terms (Clark & Dorward, 1991, pp. 13–16). Apart from the Scriptures, Augustine was "the principal source of his images and ideas" (Underhill, in Hilton, 1948, p. xviii). "A deliberately conservative Augustinianism . . . pervades his writing" (Clark, 1979, p. 204). Hilton was well-read. In the *Scale*, he referred, by name, to Augustine, Gregory, Bernard, and the Desert Fathers. In the *Episotla Aurea* he additionally named Anselm of Canterbury, Hugh of St. Victor, and Thomas Aquinas (Gardner, 1936b, p. 117). Scholars have detected further debts to John Cassian, Richard of St. Victor, William of St. Thierry, Gilbert of Hoyland, Guigo II's *Scala Claustralium*, Bonaventure, Dionysius the Areopagite (possibly at second hand), *The Cloud of Unknowing*, Richard Rolle, and William Flete's *De emendatione vitae* (Gardner, 1936b, p. 117; Underhill, in Hilton, 1948, pp. xix, xxi; Knowles, 1961, p. 104 n. 7; Clark & Doward, 1991, pp. 22–24). Hilton may also have translated William Flete's *De Remediis contra Temptaciones* into Middle English (Flete, 1968, p. 4).

Some manuscripts of *The Prickynge of Love*, the Middle English translation of *Stimulus amoris*, attribute the translation to Walter Hilton; and Hilton's original writings show debts to *The Prickynge*. In both *The Scale of Perfection* I, 92 and *The Epistle of Privy Counsel* 9, Hilton used *The Prickynge*'s idea that the humanity and passion of Christ is a door by which the soul should enter contemplation; and in both *Scale* II, 41 and *Epistle* 12, Hilton described the states of a soul in consolation and in desolation in terms derived from *The Prickynge* (Hilton, 1929, pp. li–liii; Gardner, 1933, p. 131; Clark, 1984). James of Milan's observation that "some also through grace wax ripe, so that they are all turned <<into Christ's sweetness>> without and within, and all bitterness is cut from their hearts" (Hilton, 1952, p. 163) is no less than the main theme of Book Two of *The Scale*.

THE MYSTICAL WAY IN HILTON

Academic scholarship on Hilton began during the heyday of the common core hypothesis, when mystical experiences were wrongly assumed to be everywhere one and the same (Almond, 1982). As a result, older scholarship attempted to interpret Hilton in manners that made him agree with St. John of the Cross (Sitwell, 1949–50; Pepler, 1958; du Moustier, 1959), the *Cloud of Unknowing*

(Knowles, 1961), Evelyn Underhill's interpretation of the purgative, illumina-tive, and unitive ways (Coleman, 1935, 1938; Milosh, 1966), and, in an extreme case, Hindu Yoga and the analytic psychology of Carl G. Jung (White, 1944). The tunnel vision created by the common core hypothesis led Milosh both to note that "Jesus is seen in meditation 'in a bodily likeness'" and never-theless to assert that "the cognition in the mystical experience has nothing to do with the imagination" (Milosh, 1966, p. 59). A notable exception to the reductive tendency of older scholarship was Underhill's opinion of Hilton. "Contemplation for him," she wrote, "as for St. Bernard, is simply the com-munion of love" (Underhill, 1948, p. xxvi). Hilton's differences from other mys-tics have been stressed by more recent scholarship as well (Clark, 1977, 1978a).

Hilton articulated his mystical theology within a theological framework that approached eidetic imagery with suspicion. Augustine had distinguished corporeal visions, which were perceived with the bodily senses, imaginative visions, which were apparent to the imagination; and intellectual visions, which were contemplated by the rational faculty. Hilton followed Augustine in affirming that corporeal and imaginative visions were not always reliable, whereas intellectual visions might be trusted without reservation.

> By what I have said you will to some extent understand that visions or revelations of any kind of spirit, appearing in the body or in the imagination, asleep or awake, or any other feeling in the bodily senses made in spiritual fashion—either in sound by the ear, or tasting in the mouth, or smelling to the nose, or else any heat that can be felt like fire glowing and warming the breast or any other part of the body, or anything that can be felt by bodily sense, however comforting and pleasing it may be—these are not truly contemplation. They are only simple and secondary—though they are good—compared with spiri-tual virtues and the spiritual knowledge and loving of God. (Hilton, 1991, pp. 83–84)

Again agreeing with St. Augustine, Hilton counted exclusively intellectual experiences as the third and final type of contemplation. He considered intel-lectual inspiration as an act of grace within the human intellect that accom-plishes a mystical union.

> The third part of contemplation, which is as perfect as can be here, lies both in cognition and affection: that is to say, in the knowing and per-fect loving of God. . . . he is visited and taken up from all earthly and fleshly affections, from vain thoughts and imaginations of all bodily things, and is as if forcibly ravished out of the bodily senses; and then is illumined by the grace of the Holy Spirit to see intellectually the

Truth, which is God, and also spiritual things, with a soft, sweet burning love for him—so perfectly that by the rapture of this love the soul is for the time united and conformed to the image of the Trinity. . . . St. Paul says this of such union and conforming: *Qui adhaeret Deo, unus spiritus est cum illo*. [1 Cor. 6:17: But anyone who is joined to the Lord is one spirit with Him.] That is to say, if anyone is fastened to God by the rapture of love, then God and the soul are not two, but both are one—not in flesh, but in one spirit—and certainly in this union that marriage is made between God and the soul which shall never be broken. (Hilton, 1991, p. 82)

The particular variety of spiritual experience that Hilton discussed as contemplative union was the negative theological experience advocated by Bonaventure. Hilton's phrasing, that it is an experience of knowing that God is, while also knowing that it is impossible to know what God is (Hilton, 1991, p. 259), traced through Bonaventure to the Jewish Middle Platonist, Philo of Alexandria, who wrote in the first century (Merkur, 2001a). Hilton wrote:

He [the soul] does not see what he [God] is, for no created being can do that in heaven or earth; and he [the soul] does not see him *as* he is, for that sight is only in the glory of heaven. But he sees that he is: an unchangeable being, a supreme power, supreme truth, supreme goodness; a blessed life, an endless beatitude. (Hilton, 1991, p. 259)

In the continuation of the same passage, Hilton followed Bernard of Clairvaux in emphasizing the emotional content of intellectual contemplation (p. 83).

This the soul sees, and much more that comes with it; not blindly, nakedly, and without savor, as with a scholar who sees him by his learning, only through the power of his naked reason; but he sees him through an understanding which is strengthened and illuminated by the gift of the Holy Spirit, with a wonderful reverence and a secret burning love, and with spiritual savor and heavenly delight—more clearly and more fully than may be written or told. (Hilton, 1991, p. 259)

Although it is intellectual, the comprehension that God is, is not accomplished by naked reason. It is a ravishment or rapture that involves "a wonderful reverence and a secret burning love."

Much as Hilton kept to Augustine's terminology, he applied a negative theology to the understanding of contemplation. He asserted that the soul does not directly see God in contemplation, as it will do in the beatific vision post mortem. What the soul beholds during contemplation is a "kind of seeing and knowing" (Hilton, 1991, p. 259). What the soul contemplates in this life is an understanding about God, as distinct from God himself. "As Saint John says: *Tunc videbimus eum sicuti est.* That is, then we shall see Him as He is [1 John 3:2]" (Hilton, 1991, p. 259).

Hilton extended the term "contemplation" to a variety of phenomena that had not generally been considered contemplative prior to Bonaventure. In the fourth century, Evagrius Ponticus (1981, p. 15) had approved "of the contemplation of the physical world, and . . . of the contemplation of God." The Desert Father's program remained in place as late as the twelfth century, when Hugh of St. Victor (1962, p. 184) acknowledged "two kinds of contemplation. . . . the consideration of created things . . . [and] the contemplation of the Creator." Hilton entertained a more diverse program. Contemplation, through which the soul might be "reformed to the likeness of Jesus by fullness of virtue" (Hilton, 1991, p. 83), was most commonly achieved through "the reading of holy Scripture and holy teaching, spiritual meditation, and diligent prayer with devotion" (pp. 87–88).

Having expanded the category of contemplation well beyond the two topics of monastic tradition, Hilton reconceptualized the tripartite mystical way. Far from being a progression from purgation through illumination to contemplation, Hilton's path was a progression among three types of contemplation. Hilton's first part of contemplation cultivated human understanding. It consisted of "the knowledge of God and the things of the spirit, acquired by reason, by the teaching of man and by the study of holy scripture" (Hilton, 1991, p. 79). The second part of contemplation was ethical. "A person's soul is . . . cleansed from all sins and reformed to the image of Jesus by completeness of virtues" (Hilton, 1991, p. 70; see also p. 72). Conformity with Jesus in the image of his humanity had to be achieved prior to conformity with the image of his godhood.

Speaking of the third stage of contemplation, "which is as perfect as can be here" (Hilton, 1991, p. 82), Hilton alluded to meditation on the passion: "Nobody can come to the contemplation of the Deity unless by the fullness of humility and charity he is first reformed to the likeness of Jesus in his manhood" (Hilton, 1991, p. 160; see also pp. 83, 87). It was not simply that Hilton recommended meditation on the passion prior to attempting intellectual contemplation. Hilton claimed that success at meditation on the passion was necessary before the further grace of intellectual contemplation could be expected.

Where the general Franciscan concern with a conformance to Jesus' style of life concerned monks' behavior, Hilton agreed with James of Milan in prioritizing character change that produced a Christ-like temperament of the soul.

There is many a man that has virtues, such as lowliness, patience, charity toward his fellow Christians and so on, only in his reason and will, but without any spiritual delight or love in them. Often he feels grudging, sad and bitter as he practices them, and nevertheless he does it, stirred only by reason and the fear of God. This man has virtues in his reason and will, but not the love of them in affection. But when by the grace of Jesus and by spiritual and bodily exercise the reason is turned into light and the will into love, then he has virtues in affection. . . . the virtues which were at first hard to practice are now turned into real delight and savor, as happens when someone enjoys himself in patience, humility, purity, sobriety and charity as much as in any pleasures. (Hilton, 1991, p. 87)

Because the study of Christian mysticism is a different scholarly specialty than the study of Christian devotionalism, and meditation is considered a devotion rather than part of mysticism, scholars who discuss Hilton as a mystic have not mentioned, much less appreciated, the place of meditation in his spiritual practice. Meditation on the passion goes unmentioned, for example, in Bernard McGinn's encyclopedic multivolume study of *The Presence of God: A History of Western Christian Mysticism* (1991, 1994, 1998). Specialists on devotionalism with a deepened understanding of medieval meditation have noted Hilton's concern, in his words, with "meditation on Christ's humanity and passion, on the Blessed Virgin and the saints, and on vices and virtues, the mercy of Christ and the joys of heaven" (Clark & Dorward, 1991, p. 39; see also Hussey, 1980, pp. 2–4; Glasscoe, 1993, pp. 135–36). However, the relation between Hilton's meditations and his mysticism has not been understood. Let us make an attempt to enter into Hilton's point of view.

MEDITATION IN HILTON

Hilton asserted that meditation and prayer were the means by which the soul might be conformed to the emotional temperament of Jesus.

By meditation you shall see how far you lack virtues, and by prayer you shall get them. By meditation you shall see your wretchedness, your sins and your wickedness—such as pride, covetousness, gluttony, lechery, wicked stirrings of envy, wrath, hatred, sullenness, angriness, bitterness, sloth and unreasonable worry. You will also find your heart full of vain shames and fears of your flesh and of the world. All these stirrings will always bubble out of your heart as water will run out from the spring of a stinking well, and hinder the sight of your soul from either seeing or feeling purely the love of Jesus Christ. For know well, until your heart is largely cleansed from such sins you cannot have perfectly the spiritual knowledge of God, according to his own witness in the gospel: *Beati mundo corde: quoniam ipsi Deum videbunt.* Blessed be the pure in heart, for they shall see God [Matthew 5:8]. In meditation you will also see the virtues that are necessary for you to have, such as humility, mildness, patience, righteousness, strength of spirit, temperance, peace, purity and sobriety, faith, hope and charity. In meditation you will see how good, how fair and how profitable these virtues are, and by prayer you will desire them and get them. (Hilton, 1991, p. 88)

Hilton wisely counselled that "in meditation no certain rule can be set for someone always to keep, for they are in the free gift of our Lord according to the various dispositions of chosen souls" (Hilton, 1991, p. 104). Among the different meditations that a person might pursue, Hilton emphasized meditations on Jesus' humanity and St. Mary's compassion, and he singled out meditation on the passion for an extended discussion.

Suppose you are stirred to devotion in God, and suddenly your thought is drawn up from all worldly and carnal things, and you feel as if you see in your soul your Lord appear in bodily likeness as he was on earth—how he was taken by the Jews and bound like a thief, beaten and despised, scourged and condemned to death; how humbly he bore the cross upon his back, and how cruelly He was nailed onto it; also the crown of thorns upon his head, and the sharp spear that stung him to the heart. As you see this in the spirit, you feel your heart stirred to such great compassion and pity for your Lord Jesus that you moan and weep and cry with all the powers of your body and your soul, wondering at the goodness and love, patience and humility of our Lord Jesus, that he would suffer so much pain for such a sinful as you are. And also, above this, you feel so much goodness and mercy in our Lord that your heart rises up into love and gladness for him, with many sweet tears, having great trust in the forgiveness of your sins, and in the salvation of your soul by the power of this precious passion. Then—when the remembrance of Christ's passion or any point of his humanity is thus caused in your heart by such spiritual vision, with devout affection answering to it—then, know well that it is not your own doing, neither the pretense of any wicked spirit, but by the grace of the Holy Spirit. (Hilton, 1991, p. 106)

Hilton's formulation, "the remembrance of Christ's passion . . . is . . . caused in your heart...with devout affection answering to it," expressed his view that the emotions that the soul feels during its meditations are responses by the soul to the spiritual vision. He was implicitly opposing the point of view, which has dominated Catholic practice since the Counter-Reformation, that the emotions are themselves effects of grace. If, when meditating, a person suddenly has a deeply emotional feeling, the mystical theologies of the Counter-Reformation regarded the emotion as a gift of grace, a feeling that the person was supposed to have, in order to be motivated as God willed the person to be. For Hilton, the emotions were instead human and fallible. They were not revelatory and infallible, as, for example, Ignatian spirituality today holds.

In the direct continuation of this same passage, Hilton cited Bernard and Paul as precedents for his performance of meditation on the passion prior to mystical union.

> For it is an opening of the eye of the spirit into Christ's humanity, and it may be called the carnal love of God, as St. Bernard calls it, inasmuch as it is set in the human nature of Christ. It is very good, and a great help in destroying great sins, and a way to come to virtues, and so afterward into contemplation of the divine nature. For a person shall not commonly come to spiritual delight in the contemplation of Christ's divinity unless he first comes in imagination by anguish and compassion for his humanity.
>
> This is what Saint Paul did, for first he spoke thus: *Nihil indicavi me scire inter vos nisi Jesum Christum et hunc crucifixum.* I showed you nothing at all that I knew, except only Jesus Christ, and Him crucified [1 Corinthians 2:2]; as if he had said, My knowledge and my trust are only in the passion of Christ. Therefore he also said: *Mihi autem absit gloriari nisi in cruce Domini nostri Iesu Christi.* Let every kind of joy and pleasure be forbidden me, except in the cross and passion of our Lord Jesus Christ [Galatians 6:14]. And afterward he said this, "*Praedicamus vobis Christum Dei virtutem, et Dei sapientiam*" (1 Corinthians 1:24). [We preach to you a Christ Who is the power and the wisdom of God.] As if he said, "First I preached to you of the humanity and of the passion of Christ; now I preach to you of His divinity and power, and of the endless wisdom of God." (p. 106)

In referring to "the eye of the spirit," Hilton invoked the conventional medieval concept of the "interior senses" or "inward wits" by which the soul apprehends spiritual realities in imaginative forms (Wolfson, 1935; Harvey, 1975). The concept presupposed that visions are extrasensory perceptions of spiritual realities that are apprehended by "interior senses" that belong to the imaginative faculty of the soul. The concept of "interior senses" was also used metaphorically in reference to intellectual perceptions of intelligible phenomena, such as ideas, forms, processes, and so forth. Hilton here referred literally, however, to pictorial imagination.

Hilton maintained that meditation on the passion is "a great help in destroying great sins." In this phrasing Hilton left open the question whether meditation on the passion might in individual cases be facilitated by divine grace and so become the vehicle of a contemplative state. Only lines earlier, he had asserted that "spiritual vision . . . is not your own doing . . . but by the grace of the Holy Spirit" (Hilton, 1991, p. 106). However, Hilton was implicitly aware that meditations are not always assisted by grace. Meditators may encounter periods of spiritual "dryness," and Hilton addressed his theology to the general circumstance of meditation as a whole. At the same time, Hilton explained that "a person shall not commonly come to spiritual delight in the contemplation of Christ's divinity unless he first comes in imagination by anguish and compassion for his humanity." The remark implied that an intellectual experience of grace was ordinarily attained only after having identified with both the anguish and the compassion that Jesus felt on the cross.

Hilton implicated sin in the contents of meditation on the passion. The prospect of intellectual contemplation arouses guilt in a sinful soul, and the crisis of conscience builds to the point of fearing and imagining death. However, meditation on the passion had the virtue of accomplishing "the slaying of all sin."

> Inasmuch as the soul cannot promptly find its spiritual rest in the love and sight of God, it must needs feel pain. This task is rather restricted and narrow; nevertheless, it is a way Christ taught in the gospel to those who wanted to be his perfect followers, speaking thus: *Contendite intrare per angustam portam; quoniam arcta est via quae ducit ad vitam et pauci inveniunt eam* [Luke 13:24; Matthew 7:14]. Strive to go in by the strait gate; for the way leading to heaven is narrow, and few people find it. Our Lord tells us in another place how strict this way is: *Si quis vult post me venire, abneget semetipsum, et tollat crucem suam, et sequatur me. Item qui odit animam suam in hoc mundo, in vitam aeternam custodit eam* [Matthew 16:24; John 12:25: If anyone wants to be a follower of mine, let him renounce himself and take up his cross and follow me. For anyone who wants to save his life will lose it; but anyone who loses his life for my sake will find it.] That is to say, whoever wants to come after me, forsake himself and hate his own soul (that is to say, abandon all fleshly love, and hate all his own fleshly life and the feeling of his body through all his senses, for love of me); and take cross (that is to say, suffer the pain of this a while); and then follow (that is to say, into contemplation of me).
>
> This is a strait and narrow way, so that no bodily thing can pass through it; for it is the slaying of all sins, as St. Paul says: *Mortificate*

membra vestra quae sunt super terram: immunditiam, libidinem, concu-
piscentiam malam [Colossians 3:5: That is why you must kill everything in you that belongs only to earthly life: fornication, impurity,
guilty passion, evil desires, and especially greed.] Put to death your
limbs on earth: not the parts of your body, but of the soul, such as
impurity, lust and unreasonable love for yourself and earthly things.
(Hilton, 1991, p. 113)

Hilton's language, his citation of Scripture, and his list of vices owed much
to conventional preaching; but he used traditional Christian language to
express an enduring truth of dynamic psychotherapy. Unless a patient goes into
the area of pain, with its shame, guilt, misery, sorrow, and regret, a restructur-
ing of the personality is not possible.

Hilton did not suggest that affection for virtues was easily acquired. He
urged people to persevere in virtue through knowledge or reason, even when
affection was lacking.

If you cannot feel this humility in your heart with affection, as you
wish, do what you can: humble yourself in will by your reason . . .
regarding yourself as a worse wretch in that you cannot truly feel what
you are; and if you do so, although your flesh rises against it and will
not assent to your will, do not be too frightened, but bear and suffer
the false feeling of your flesh as a punishment. (Hilton, 1991, p. 92)

Where Greek and Latin Christianity have traditionally conceptualized
the monk as a spiritual athlete, who throughout his life is constantly engaged
in training and competition (Blum & Golitzin, 1991), or a spiritual warrior
engaged in unending battle (Scupoli, 1945), Hilton thought otherwise. He
required ethical behavior even when its motivation was conflicted; but he
claimed that inner conflict between the spirit and the flesh was expectable only
at the beginning of the mystical path. Internal conflict over spirituality was not
necessarily a lifelong preoccupation.

Hilton's reference to "the false feeling of your flesh" drew on the traditional Christian language that attributed sinful wishes to the flesh. He
described people who attempt to be humble but do not feel humble. What they
actually feel is opposite to how they think of themselves. What Hilton meant
by "false feeling" may consequently be recognized, in psychoanalytic terms, as
a "reaction-formation," a circumstance in which one's conscious feelings and
motives are the precise opposite of preconscious feelings and motives.

If you do not believe me, test yourself. If you have love and delight in
the having and holding of anything that you own, such as it is, and

feed your heart with this love for a time; or if you have a desire and yearning to possess something that you do not have, and through this desire your heart is troubled and vexed with undue concern, so that the pure desire of virtues and of God cannot rest within it: this is a sign that there is covetousness in this image. And if you want to make a better proof, notice if anything that you have is taken away from you by force, by borrowing, or in any other way, so that you cannot get it again, and you are distressed, angered and troubled over it in your heart, both because you lack the thing which you want and cannot, and also because you are moved against the person who has it, to contend and quarrel with him over his unwillingness to restore it again when he could. This is a sign that you love worldly goods. (Hilton, 1991, p. 142)

Hilton was not describing conscious hypocrisy. He was discussing "false feeling," a conscious attitude that was falsified by behavior and feelings that were not ordinarily associated with it.

Hilton's psychologically astute way of understanding people in terms of inconsistent feelings informed an observation about people who achieve ease in avoiding sinful behavior, but without reforming in feeling.

Some people who are reformed in faith at the beginning of their turning to God set themselves in a certain kind of exercise (whether of body or of spirit) and think always to keep to that way of working, and not to change it for any other that comes through grace, even though it were better, for they suppose that practice always to be best for them to keep, and therefore they rest in it, and so bind themselves to it by habit that when they have completed it they feel wonderfully at ease, thinking they have done a great thing for God; and if it happens by chance that they are hindered from their custom, they are angry and despondent—even though it may be for a reasonable cause—and their conscience is as troubled as if they had done a great mortal sin. To some degree these people hinder themselves from feeling more grace, for they set their perfection in a bodily work, and so they make an end in the middle of the way, where there is no end. (Hilton, 1991, p. 222)

Hilton noted an abrupt shift from feeling wonderfully at ease in the security of routine religious practices, to anger, despondence, and a severely troubled conscience upon the routine's disruption. The emotional shift revealed the false perfection of the ease they took in their practice. In psychoanalytic terms, we might credit Hilton with having described denial and the inability to maintain it.

Conformance to the temperament of Jesus through the cultivation of affection for virtue was to be achieved, with the help of Jesus, by coming first to recognize the extent of the image of sin within oneself, and secondly by destroying it.

> Then begin, and break this image. When you have inwardly considered yourself and your wretchedness as I have said—how proud, how envious and resentful, how covetous, how carnal and how full of corruption you are; also how little knowledge, feeling, or savor you have of God, and how wise and lively you are in your savor of earthly things, so that in short you feel yourself to be as full of sin as the skin is full of flesh—although you think of yourself in this way, do not be too frightened. When you have done this, lift up the desire of your heart to your Lord Jesus and pray to him for help; cry to him with great desires and sighings, that he will help you to bear the heavy burden of this image, or else that he will break it. (Hilton, 1991, p. 157)

> Do as I have said, and better if you can, and by the grace of Jesus I think you will make the devil ashamed, and so break away these wicked stirrings that they shall not do you much harm; and in this manner that image of sin can be broken down in you and destroyed, by which you are deformed from the natural shape of the image of Christ. You shall be formed again to the image of the man Jesus by humility and charity, and then you shall be fully shaped to the image of Jesus God, living here in a shadow by contemplation, and in the glory of heaven by the fullness of truth. (Hilton, 1991, p. 159)

Hilton's general advice may be assumed to have been addressed to meditators on all topics and at all levels of proficiency. In several passages, however, Hilton indicated that meditation on the passion was the particular meditation through which the image of sin might be broken. Citing Matthew 16:24, "If anyone wants to be a follower of mine, let him renounce himself and take up his cross and follow me," Hilton commented, "This is a strait and narrow way, so that no bodily thing can pass through it; for it is the slaying of all sins" (Hilton, 1991, p. 113). The same passage continued with the instruction, "take cross...and then follow (that is to say, into contemplation)," which implies that taking the cross was to be done in meditation. In a later passage Hilton (1991) wrote:

> Then what are you to do with this image? I answer you with the word that the Jews spoke to Pilate about Christ: *Tolle, Tolle, crucifige eum!* [John 19:15: Take him away! Take him away! Crucify him!] Take this

body of sin and put it upon the cross. That is to say, Break down this image and slay the false love of sin in yourself. (p. 156)

The language in this passage had a long history of allegorical use in reference to self-control and mortification by those beginning the religious life. Hilton likely intended his words to apply simultaneously to new religious and to advanced practitioners of meditation. His words were deliberately equivocal in order that each audience be able to interpret his words in a manner that was appropriate to their stage of development.

Hilton did not suggest that meditation on the passion was inherently transformative. "A person does not always have this kind of meditation when he would, but when our Lord wants to give it" (Hilton, 1991, pp. 107–8). A person who meditated on the passion might imagine death vividly, but it was only when grace facilitated the mental imaging that it developed into a contemplative state that functioned experientially as a death of sin.

Writing of the "spiritual delight" (Hilton, 1991, p. 156) that follows the contemplative experience, Hilton warned against the possibilities of spiritual pride and false self-confidence. Where James of Milan had described inflation that followed contemplative experience, Hilton discussed the particular use of inflation that Kleinian object relations theory terms "the manic defense" (Winnicott, 1935):

> If he cannot hamper him by obvious bodily sins he would like to hinder and beguile him by this vanity of bodily savors or sweetness in the senses, so as to bring him into spiritual pride and false self-confidence. This soul supposes himself to have by it a feeling of heavenly joy, and thinks he is half in paradise for the delight that he feels all about him, when he is nearly at hell's gates, and so by pride and presumption he can fall into errors or fantasies, or into other bodily or spiritual calamities. (Hilton, 1991, pp. 84–85)

Hilton warned against a blithely cheerful euphoria that coincides with oblivion to the shame, guilt, sorrow and regret that a realistic self-appraisal would demand.

Only an ecstasy that furthered the general religious life was to be trusted as a gift from God:

> Though it [meditative experience] may upset you when it first begins to come, nonetheless afterward it turns and quickens your heart to greater desire for virtues, and increases your love both for God and for your fellow Christians. Also it makes you humbler in your own sight. By these tokens you may know that it is from God. (Hilton, 1991, p. 85)

With these words, Hilton described the stage of therapeutic progress that Melanie Klein (1935, 1937, 1940) termed "the depressive position" and D. W. Winnicott (1948, 1950–55, 1952, 1954–55) called the "stage of concern." Sorrow and regret, pertaining to one's own experiences and actions, are followed by a concern with others, humility, and the loving will to make reparation.

Reforming in Feeling

The chapters of *The Scale of Perfection* are organized in two books, and it is probable that some years elapsed between Hilton's composition of the two sections. Book I is addressed to an anchoress; it contains almost all of Hilton's efforts to deploy Augustine's theology of the image of sin and the image of God. One may imagine that it was composed shortly after Hilton joined the Augustinian Canons at Thurgarton and was concerned to demonstrate his technical proficiency at the theological tradition of Augustine, Bernard, and Bonaventure. Book II, by contrast, is addressed to both recluses and contemplatives who pursued a mixed life. It seems the work of a seasoned spiritual director, confident of the validity of his teachings, who favors simple and plainspoken words that will communicate his ideas effectively to lay people. Gardner (1936a, p. 14) suggested that Book II was originally intended as a separate, self-contained work; it certainly presents significant advances in Hilton's thinking. It was here that he presented his ideas on reforming in feeling.

At the very beginning of Book II, Hilton announced his purpose to translate the technical concepts of scholastic theology into a popular vocabulary that we may describe as psychological. Referring to the image of God, Hilton wrote:

> If you want to know plainly what I mean by it, I tell you truthfully that I understand nothing else but your own soul, for your soul, my soul, and every rational soul is an image, and an honorable one at that, since it is the image of God. (Hilton, 1991, p. 193)

In the second chapter of Book II, Hilton justified his topic by drawing attention to a fact of common Christian experience. Fulfilling the commandment to love God does not reform the soul to the image of God that it possessed before Adam's fall. The reverse is true. Loving God is not fully possible until the soul has reformed (Hilton, 1991, p. 194).

Hilton suggested that the full reformation of the soul awaited the beatific vision post-mortem. The reforming that was possible during mortal life was never more than partial. There were two kinds of partial reforming. Hilton termed them "reforming in faith" and "reforming in faith and in feeling"

(Hilton, 1991, p. 200). Reforming in faith was a well-known concept with a well-defined place in Christian theology. It was the experience Augustine had called the restoration of the image of God. "Reforming in faith and in feeling" was Hilton's original teaching. To justify his innovation, he developed the term through a paraphrase of Romans 12:2, wherein Paul had written of the abandonment of sin through a change of feeling.

> So that you do not take as pretense or fantasy this way in which I speak of the soul's reforming in feeling, I shall base it upon St. Paul's words, where he speaks like this. *Nolite conformari huic saeculo, sed reformamini in novitate sensus vestri.* That is, You who are through grace reformed in faith, do not henceforth conform yourselves to the manners of the world in pride, covetousness or other sins, but be reformed in newness of feeling [Romans 12:2]. Look, here you can see that St. Paul speaks of reforming in feeling; and what that new feeling is he explains in another place like this: *Ut impleamini in agnitione voluntatis eius, in omni intellectu et sapientia spirituali.* That is, We pray God that you may be filled with knowledge of God's will in all understanding and in every kind of spiritual wisdom [Colossians 1:9]. This is reforming in feeling. (Hilton, 1991, pp. 257–58)

The distinction clarified an important detail that Hilton had not made explicit in Book I of the *Scale.* How may people, through grace, have faith in God and be saved, and according to Augustine have the image of God restored within them, and yet they commit sins? To explain away the problem, Augustine had opted for a distinction between the image and likeness of God (Bell, 1984, pp. 30–33, 42–44). Hilton, who wrote after the scholastic turn to nominalism, instead based himself on the lived realities of religious experience:

> The first, which is reforming in faith alone. . . . may be gained easily and in a short time; the second not so, but through length of time and great spiritual labor. The first can be had together with the feeling of the image of sin, for though a man feels nothing in himself, but all stirrings of sin and fleshly desires, notwithstanding that feeling, if he does not deliberately assent to it he may be reformed in faith to the likeness of God. But the second reforming drives out the enjoyment and feeling of fleshly stirrings and worldly desires and allows no such spots to remain in this image. The first reforming is only for souls beginning and proficient, and for people in active life; the second is for perfect souls and contemplatives. By the first reforming the image of sin is not destroyed, but is left as if all whole in feeling; but the second reforming destroys the old feelings of this image of sin and brings

into the soul new gracious feelings through the working of the Holy Spirit. The first is good; the second is better. (Hilton, 1991, pp. 199–200)

Christians embraced the same set of virtues and vices whether they were reformed in faith, or reformed in faith and feeling. Meditators had all achieved faith and been baptized before they began to meditate. They had all adopted one or another form of the Christian life. The virtues toward which they formally aspired were unaffected by their reformations in feeling. Reforming in feeling changed their emotional orientations toward their values. Instead of "false feelings," they were freed of "the old feelings of this image of sin." The change in feelings altered meditators' capacities to live up to the values that they espoused. Virtues that they had experienced as impositions on their character, necessitating spiritual athletics or spiritual warfare, could, through reforming in faith and feeling, instead be experienced as uncomplicated, free desires. When virtue ceased to be a struggle and instead acquired the ease of being "second nature," a person was reformed in feeling. Reforming in feeling brought people to increased compassion both for themselves and for others, in conformance with the sweetness of Jesus.

Because reforming in faith "can be had together with the feeling of the image of sin," we may describe it as a condition of mental conflict. In support of his claim of the insufficiency of "reforming in faith," Hilton appealed to sacramental theology. Reforming in faith restored the image of God, but to so little an extent that contrition, the sacrament of confession, and penance remained necessary (Hilton, 1991, pp. 202–3). In *Eight Chapters on Perfection*, Hilton's Middle English translation of a lost Latin treatise by Lluis de Fontibus, the text states:

> When you are tortured with trouble or temptation, make frequent use of confession as well as prayer: in this you will show your confessor, with full contrition of your heart, completely and honestly, all the wounds of your conscience, great and small, as extensively as you would show them to your own angel. This is a sovereign medicine for getting rid of temptations and troubles and obtaining the great grace of God's comfort. (Hilton, 1983, pp. 3–4)

"Getting rid of temptations" temporarily was possible through penance. For those who were reformed only in faith, life was a constant struggle against sin:

> He needs always to be striving and fighting against wicked stirrings from this image of sin, and to make no agreement or friendship with

it, to be obedient to its irrational biddings, for if he does he deceives himself. (Hilton, 1991, pp. 207–8)

Reforming in feeling differed. It "destroys the old feelings of this image of sin and brings into the soul new gracious feelings through the working of the Holy Spirit" (Hilton, 1991, p. 200). It transformed contrition from a momentary achievement in the presence of a confessor, to a stable component within the personality. What was at stake theologically in this assertion? For Augustine, all that was to be achieved in this life was a cleansing of the image of God, which he defined as the soul's rational faculty. Nothing more was to be achieved than a cognitive transformation. As long as the soul remained in the body of flesh, it would have desires, and those desires would keep alive a residue of the image of sin (Bell, 1984, pp. 30–33). A Christian was to aim at *apatheia*, an imperturbable equanimity that was indifferent to the flesh. Critical of mere intellectualism, Bernard had instead emphasized that the spiritual marriage consists of love as well as knowledge (Merkur, 2001a, pp. 60–65); and Hilton concluded that the perfection possible in this life, which according to Augustine occurs during contemplation of God, necessarily entails a reformation of feeling in addition to a purification of reason. In Middle English, the term "felyng" or "felynge" might refer to sensations or emotions; it might also be a synonym of understanding, contemplation, and vision in Augustine's sense of the term (Cleve, 1994, p. 49).

Laboring with the common core hypothesis of mystical experience, Sitwell (1953) concluded that "reforming in feeling" was not a euphemism for contemplation. For Hilton "the union between God and the soul effected by sanctifying grace. . . . *reforms* the soul in the image of God" (p. xi). Hilton defended the traditional view that the soul achieves such perfection as is possible during mortal life when it contemplates God. However, Hilton privileged contemplation because it serves to reform the soul in feeling. It was not for its own sake, but for its fruit, that Hilton valued contemplation.

> In this way Love works in a soul, opening the spiritual eye to gaze upon Jesus by the inspiration of special grace, and making it pure, subtle and fit for the work of contemplation. . . . This opening of the spiritual eyes is that luminous darkness and rich nothing . . . and it may be called *purity of spirit and spiritual rest, inward stillness and peace of conscience, highness of thought and solitude of soul, a lively feeling of grace and secrecy of heart, the waking sleep of the spouse and tasting of heavenly savor, burning in love and shining in light, entrance to contemplation and reforming in feeling. . . .*
>
> For a soul that through the visitation of grace has one, has all, because when a soul sighing to see the face of Jesus is touched

through special grace of the Holy Spirit, it is suddenly changed and turned from the plight that it was in to another way of feeling. It is wonderfully separated from the love and pleasure of all earthly things and drawn first into itself, so much that it has lost the savor of bodily life and of everything that is, save only Jesus. And *then it is clean from all the filth of sin*, so far that the memory of it and all inordinate affection for any creature is suddenly washed and wiped away, so that there is no obstacle in the middle between Jesus and the soul, but only the life of the body. And *then it is in spiritual rest*, because all painful doubts and fears and all other temptations of spiritual enemies are driven out of the heart, so that they do not trouble it or sink into it for the time. It is at rest from the annoyance of worldly business and the painful vexation of wicked stirrings, but it is very busy in the free spiritual work of love, and the more it labors, the more rest it feels.

This restful labor is very far from idleness of the flesh and from false confidence. It is full of spiritual work, yet it is called rest, because grace loosens the heavy yoke of carnal love from the soul, making it strong and free through the gift of spiritual love, in order to work gladly, gently and with delight in everything where it is stirred to work by grace. (Hilton, 1991, pp. 280–81)

Clark (1978b) concluded:

Hilton is emphatic that, though 'reforming in feeling' may be a habitual state, the 'lively feeling of grace' which makes doing the will of God joyful and spontaneous comes and goes. While it lasts serious sin is impossible. (p. 76)

Reforming in faith and feeling could occur temporarily during an ecstatic rapture, but Hilton maintained that its more permanent acquisition was attained "through long toil and great effort. . . . after great abundance of grace and great spiritual labor" (Hilton, 1991, p. 219). The occurrence of spiritual experiences was no guarantee that a person had been reformed in feeling. Beginners often had dramatic spiritual experiences because they overreacted to the experiences they were given (Hilton, 1991, pp. 250–51). Like James of Milan, Hilton was equally skeptical of the value of ecstatic gifts, such as prophesy, speaking in tongues, and so forth. In Hilton's view, gifts were unrelated to reforming in feeling. The occurrence of gifts was no indication that reforming in feeling had been accomplished (Hilton, 1991, p. 269). Hilton was so far from seeing spiritual experiences as a proof of completed reforming, as to characterize them as a sort of spiritual food whose nourishment of the soul was necessary to sustain the soul during the labor of the second stage (Hilton, 1991, pp. 251–52).

Clark and Dorward (1991) explained: "Reforming in feeling means that the power of the old impulses is broken. This pertains to 'perfect' souls" (p. 43). Hilton wrote:

> When he is first healed of his spiritual sickness, when all bitter passions, carnal pleasures and other old feelings are burnt out of the heart with the fire of desire, and new gracious feelings are brought in, with burning love and spiritual light: then a soul draws near to perfection and to reforming in feeling. (Hilton, 1991, p. 219)

The traditional conceptualization of the soul's progress as a movement toward mystical union can be found in Hilton's writings, but his interest was in the soul's reformation. Claiming that "St. Paul divides our Lord's work into four times" (Hilton, 1991, p. 248), Hilton presented a four-stage model of the soul's progress. Reforming began with the eager and confident optimism of a convert newly reformed in faith (Hilton, 1991, p. 248). Next came the difficult work of changing one's customary behavior in sober earnest. The process is conflicted and temptation severe. The convert "feels great hindrance both inside himself . . . and from without" (Hilton, 1991, p. 248). The third stage is the achievement of the full measure of reforming in faith and feeling that is possible in this life. "The third time [is] of magnifying, and this is when the soul is partly reformed in feeling, and receives the gift of perfection and the grace of contemplation; and that is a time of great rest" (Hilton, 1991, p. 249). The fourth stage is the complete reforming postmortem. "And after this comes the fourth time, of glorifying. That is when the soul shall be fully reformed in the bliss of heaven" (Hilton, 1991, p. 249).

In Hilton's presentation, reforming in feeling might be experienced either during an ecstasy or during normal waking sobriety. Hilton regarded reforming in feeling as a greater good than contemplation; but because it occurred during contemplation, Hilton was able to endorse Augustine's view that contemplation was the greatest perfection that is possible in this life. Quoting Ephesians 4:23–24, "Your mind must be renewed by a spiritual revolution, so that you can put on the new self that has been created in God's way, in the goodness and holiness of the truth," Hilton commented:

> Be renewed in the spirit of your soul. That is, you are to be reformed, not in bodily feeling or in imagination, but in the higher part of your reason, and clothe yourselves in a new man, who is created according to God, in righteousness. That is, your reason, which is properly the image of God through grace of the Holy Spirit, shall be clothed in a new light of truth, holiness and righteousness, and then it is reformed in feeling. For when the soul has

perfect knowledge of God, then is it reformed (Hilton, 1991, p. 258).

Where Augustine had maintained that the soul attains perfect spirituality when it contemplates God, who is perfect spirit; Bernard had added that the soul attains perfect love when it contemplates God, who is love; and Hilton endorsed Bernard's formulation. Hilton equated reforming in feeling with contemplation of God not because contemplation reduced the soul to pure knowledge, but because God is love.

> The gift of love is the Holy Spirit, God Himself, and no soul can have Him and also be damned, because that gift alone saves it from damnation and makes it God's son, a partner in the heavenly heritage. That love, as I have said before, is not the affection of love that is created in a soul, but it is the Holy Spirit himself—Love uncreated— who saves a soul. (Hilton, 1991, p. 269)

Conforming with Love uncreated, the soul was reformed not only in faith but also in feeling.

What Hilton described as reforming in feeling was, in my opinion, the psychological phenomenon that the psychoanalyst Marjorie Brierley (1951) termed "psychic integration." Brierley distinguished two types of integration: (a) an integration of the ego and the superego, such as was the goal of the Christian monastic life; and (b) an integration of the id, ego, and superego, which represents the optimal aspiration according to psychoanalysis. Brierley's second type of integration corresponds to the better known term, "self-actualization," which the humanistic psychologist Abraham Maslow (1968) defined, among other manners, as "a fusion of ego, id, super-ego and ego-ideal" (p. 96). Hans Loewald (1980) regarded psychic integration as the goal of a successful psychoanalysis. Nancy McWilliams (1994) wrote:

> People have a natural feel for the difference between behavior change that is possible in spite of one's psychology and behavior change that has come to feel congruent with one's insides. To move from the first to the second condition is one reason patients often choose to stay in analytic treatment for the long haul. An analogy would be the difference that a man addicted to alcohol feels between early sobriety, during which he struggles minute by minute to resist the temptation to drink, and later recovery, when he no longer feels the urge. The *behavior* of not drinking is the same in early and late sobriety, but the underpinnings of it change. It may have taken years of AA meetings and unremitting discipline to alter old patterns, habits, and beliefs,

but to the recovering alcoholic the shift from a barely controlled compulsion to an indifference toward alcohol is a priceless achievement. (p. 70)

Some religious conversion experiences have been interpreted as instances of psychic integration (Merkur, 1995–96; 1998b; 1999, pp. 125–38). According to Haartman (2004), a dramatic increase in psychic integration was the nature of the experience that John Wesley termed "sanctification." Early Methodists produced the phenomena through a combination of two types of meditation. Wesley termed the first "watching"; the second, which he termed "praying," was the practice of the sense of the presence of God (see also: Oakland, 1974). Mildly increased psychic integration has also been noted as a statistically significant psychological effect of both Ignatian spirituality (Sacks, 1979) and seven-day Buddhist vipassana meditation (Emavardhana & Tori, 1997).

Hilton apparently intended both types of integration that Brierley discussed. Hilton maintained that reforming in feeling could be achieved by contemplatives whether they lived contemplative lives or instead engaged in a mixed life that was partly contemplative and otherwise active in worldly affairs (Beale, 1975; Clark, 1979). Gregory the Great and Thomas Aquinas had provided theological sanction to a mixed life in which action is not a distraction from contemplation but instead flows from it (Clark, 1979, p. 267). The military orders, Franciscan and Dominican friars, Augustinian Canons, and other clergy had been leading mixed lives since the early twelfth century (Russell-Smith, 1959, pp. 136-37); and Anselm of Havelberg advocated the mixed life of service and contemplation as preferable to the contemplative life alone (Bynum, 1973, p. 6). However, the concept's advancement as an aspiration for laity was Hilton's innovation. Hilton recommended a mixed life to secular knights, squires, merchants, and ploughmen (Clark, 1979, p. 265).

Concluding Reflections

For both contemplatives and practitioners of a mixed life, Hilton made the claim that repeatedly dying with Christ through meditation on the passion could, with the help of divine grace, bring about reforming in feeling. Hilton's originality was considerable. More than any other medieval writer, he redefined the goal of the mystical life. In his view, the goal was not "a lively feeling of grace" during mystical experiences but the reforming in faith and feeling that a lively feeling of grace made possible. Far from being an end in itself, contemplation was a means to a greater end. Reforming in faith brought with it a renunciation of sin, the will to practice virtue, and a continuing experience of struggle with temptation. When both faith and feeling were reformed, the prospect of sin lost its temptation, and a person achieved such perfection as is possible in this life.

There can be no doubt as to Hilton's reliance on meditation on the passion. Consider, for example, the implication of a casual passing reference to meditation on the passion in *Angel's Song*, a small treatise in which Hilton discussed the problem of being seduced by experiences of "spiritual sound and sweet singing" (Hilton, 1983, p. 19).

> Some men are deceived in this matter by their own imagination or by the trick of the enemy. Someone who has toiled for a long time in body and spirit to destroy sins and acquire virtues, and who has perhaps by grace obtained a little rest and a clear conscience, at once stops praying, reading Holy Scripture, meditating on the passion of Christ and considering his own wretchedness: before being called by God he violently gathers his wits together to seek out and gaze upon heavenly things with an eye not yet made spiritual by grace. (Hilton, 1983, p. 18)

Hilton counted meditation on the passion third after prayer and reading Scripture as his principle means of devotion. Hilton's treatise on *The Mixed Life* was equally emphatic. Hilton recommended that "thou mayest have mind of the manhood of our Lord in his birth and in his passion, or in any of his works, and feed thy thought with ghostly imaginations of it, for to stir thine affections more to love of him" (Hilton, 1929, p. 56). Hilton warned, however: "If devotion come not with mind of the Passion, strive not nor press not too much thereafter, and take easily that will come, and go forth to some other thought" (Hilton, 1929, p. 57). Either meditation on the passion would be efficacious, or deep devotion was not to be expected.

Hilton's claim that meditation on the passion can bring about what we may recognize as psychic integration was not a theological speculation. James of Milan noted that meditation on the passion sometimes inadvertently brought about what we may describe as dramatic resolutions of inner conflict. In *The Scale of Perfection*, Hilton presented his ideas on how transformation "into Christ's sweetness" might be produced, with God's grace, through deliberate design. His account of reforming in faith and feeling pioneered the description and theory of psychic integration in Western culture. Unless Hilton was able to produce the results that he claimed, he would not have known how to describe psychic integration so very convincingly. We are obliged to assume that he depended on empirical observations.

But how did he produce his results?

Chapter 3

Meditation on the Passion

Historians of Christianity have documented widely spread practices of devotion to Jesus in the High Middle Ages (Noye et al., 1974; Kieckhefer, 1984). Among the many kinds of devotion, scholars have noted a tradition of meditating on the death and resurrection of Jesus (Wakelin, 1980, pp. 41–44,48; Despres, 1989; Bestul, 1996). Meditations had been performed in Christianity from an early period and the techniques were transmitted from the Desert Fathers of late antiquity to the anchorites and monasteries of the Middle Ages. The Rule of St. Benedict required daily readings of biblical texts, and monks and nuns traditionally meditated on the scriptures as they were being read (Hall, 1988; Bianchi, 1998; Pennington, 1998). Special meditations on the topic of the death and resurrection of Jesus may conceivably have been taught and performed for centuries as an oral tradition that surrounded the passion narratives in Scripture. However, the earliest surviving reference to meditation on the passion dates to 1080, when the practice was recommended in Goscelin's *Liber confortarius (Book of Consolation)* as a means to incite love for the suffering Christ (Salter, 1974, pp. 135–36). The production of an independent genre of devotional literature followed soon afterward.

The oldest extant literary example of a meditation on the passion occurs in a verse prayer of St. Anselm of Canterbury (c. 1033-1109). In a "Prayer to Christ," Anselm wrote:

> . . . as much as I can, though not as much as I ought,
>   I am mindful of your passion,
> your buffeting, your scourging, your cross, your wounds,
>   how you were slain for me,

how prepared for burial and buried;
and also I remember your glorious Resurrection,
    and wonderful Ascension.
All this I hold with unwavering faith,
    and weep over the hardship of exile,
hoping in the sole consolation of your coming,
ardently longing for the glorious contemplation of your face.
(Anselm, 1973, p. 95)

Anselm's phrasing, "I remember your glorious Resurrection," strikes the modern ear oddly. How might a man in the eleventh century remember an event that occurred over a thousand years earlier? Anselm's word choice was determined by the conventional theory of meditation in the Middle Ages. Meditation was understood to be an active, voluntary process of thinking. "Meditation," wrote Hugh of St. Victor (1962, p. 183), "is the concentrated and judicious reconsideration of thought, that tries to unravel something complicated or scrutinizes something obscure to get at the truth of it." Meditation was both conceptual and imagistic. In order to reflect deeply, medieval thinkers habitually cultivated mental images that illustrated their ideas. Consider the following narrative from Eadmer's *Vita Anselmi*, a twelfth century text:

[Anselm could] see into and unravel many most obscure and previously insoluble questions about the divinity of God and about our faith. . . . Hence he applied his whole mind to this end, that according to his faith he might be found worthy to see with the eye of reason those things in the Holy Scripture which, as he felt, lay hidden in a deep obscurity. Thus one night it happened that he was lying awake on his bed before matins exercised in mind about these matters; and as he meditated he tried to puzzle out how the prophets of old could see both past and future as if they were present and set them forth beyond doubt in speech or writing.

And behold, while he was thus absorbed and striving with all his might to understand this problem, he fixed his eyes on the wall and—right through the masonry of the church and dormitory—he saw the monks whose office it was to prepare for matins going about the altar and other parts of the church lighting the candles. (as cited in Erickson, 1976, p. 42)

The image of seeing through walls provided Anselm with an analogy or metaphor for seeing through time, that permitted a difficult abstract concept to be comprehended in a simple vivid image.

Visualizing meditations as imagery helped medieval thinkers explore their ideas and especially their feelings for the topics of their meditations. Because they regarded imagination as a clothing of ideas in images that originated as sense perceptions, they considered the meditations and visualizations to be recollections that were produced by memory and the rational faculty. A person who, for example, visualized an event from the life of Jesus was consequently said to have recollected or remembered it. Strictly speaking, memories from the person's own life were remembered, but they were remembered in combinations that imaginatively portrayed an event from the life of Jesus. The term "recollection" carefully and emphatically avoided confusion with the concept of "vision." Verbal thinking and mental imaging were understood to be human acts that were within the soul's natural power to will. The distinction between natural and supernatural images was ontological. Medieval Christians regarded visions sometimes as extrasensory perceptions and sometimes as figurative or symbolic revelations, but in neither case as products of human imagination. Experiences that mental imaging could cause or induce were necessarily not grace. They might be assisted by grace, but they were not themselves grace. What could be visualized voluntarily was necessarily not a vision but a meditation (Carruthers, 1998, pp. 1–170).

In Anselm's practice of meditation on the passion, ideas and mental images were used to recollect Jesus' passion, with the goal of acquiring understanding through empathy, sorrow, guilt, wonderment, and gratitude. The references to memory kept meditators aware that no matter how deeply involved they became in their meditations, no matter how divine grace might help shape the mental images and their own emotional responses to them, the images remained constructs of their own memories, based on their own lives, and did not constitute actual visions either of past events in the Holy Land, or of present events in Heaven.

Interestingly, the psychological understanding of mental imagery that was expressed by the term "recollection" was not restricted to Christianity. It was a general legacy of the psychological theories of ancient Hellenism. The Arabic term *dhikr*, which became the technical term for meditation in Muslim Sufism (Hodgson, 1974, pp. 211–13), literally means "to remember"; and rabbinic references to "remembering the Name [of God]" likely pertained to a practice of meditation among Jews (Elliot R. Wolfson, 1999, personal communication).

In the present connection, I would like to draw attention to a further detail in Anselm's meditation on the passion. A few lines later in his poem, Anselm made it clear that he meditated on the passion of Jesus from the perspective of Jesus' mother Mary:

Why, O my soul . . .
....

Why did you not share
the sufferings of the most pure virgin,
his worthy mother and your gentle lady? (Anselm, 1973, p. 95)

In meditating on later events in the gospel narrative, Anselm took the perspectives of other eyewitnesses of the passion: Joseph of Arimathea, who took Jesus down from the cross and buried him; and the women who met angels in the tomb and learned of Jesus' resurrection (Anselm, 1973, pp. 96–97).

The Anselmian practice of meditation on the passion from the imagined perspectives of eyewitnesses was continued through the fifteenth century and beyond, among others, by Aelred of Rievaulx and St. Edmund Rich of Canterbury, in *The Wooing of Our Lord*, the *Meditationes vitae Christi*, attributed to Johannes de Caulibus, vernacular adaptations of the latter, such as *The Privity of the Passion*, by Marguerite Porete (d. 1310), Richard Rolle (c. 1300–1349), the Monk of Farne, and Julian of Norwich (1342–after 1416), and in *Ancrene Wisse, The Festis and the Passion of Oure Lord Ihesu Crist, Contemplations of the Dread and Love of God*, and other works. The practice was given its continuing form in *The Spiritual Exercises* of St. Ignatius of Loyola (1491–1556), who founded the Society of Jesus (Aelred, 1957; Rich, 1905; Savage & Watson, 1991; Ragusa, 1961; Baker, 1999; Porete, 1993; Rolle, 1988; Madigan, 1978; Monk of Farne, 1961; Julian, 1978; Pollard, 1987; Boenig, 1990; Ignatius, 1963).

LECTIO DIVINA

Meditations on the passion were presumably subject to variation, not only in their contents, but also in the techniques of meditation. In *The Ladder of Monks*, Guigo II, a Carthusian monk who died in 1188, wrote the most detailed medieval instructions that we possess for the practice of meditation on Scripture. Guigo also wrote *Twelve Meditations* which include meditations on the passion that were implicitly produced through the procedures that Guigo taught in *The Ladder of Monks*.

Fourth and fifth century patristic writers, such as St. Jerome, St. Ambrose, St. Augustine, and St. Hilary, used the terms *lectio divina* (divine reading) and *lectio sacra* (sacred reading) in connection with the reading of Scripture (Magrassi, 1998, p. 15); and St. Benedict required monks to devote perhaps more time to reading Scripture than to any other single waking activity. *Lectio divina* was eclipsed in the Counter-Reformation by other techniques of meditation, of which Loyola's *Spiritual Exercises* are preeminent; but *lectio divina* has continued as a living practice down to the present day among Benedictines and Cistercians (Trappists), who have seen to its revival since the 1970s. The points of affinity between *lectio divina* and Ignatian spirituality suggest a historical development from the one to the other.

The medieval reading of Scripture was traditionally described "by an ascending series of terms: reading, reflection, study, meditation, prayer, contemplation (in Latin: *lectio, cogitatio, studium, meditatio, oratio, contemplatio*)." Guigo included reflection and study within meditation (Magrassi, 1998, p. 104), and he explained *lectio divina* in terms of four procedures: "reading, meditation, prayer and contemplation" (Guigo, 1978, p. 68).

> Reading is the careful study of the Scriptures, concentrating all one's powers on it. Meditation is the busy application of the mind to seek with the help of one's own reason for knowledge of hidden truth. Prayer is the heart's devoted turning to God to drive away evil and obtain what is good. Contemplation is when the mind is in some sort lifted up to God and held above itself, so that it tastes the joys of everlasting sweetness. . . . Reading comes first, and is, as it were, the foundation; it provides the subject matter we must use for meditation. Meditation considers more carefully what is to be sought after; it digs, as it were, for treasure which it finds and reveals, but since it is not in meditation's power to seize upon the treasure, it directs us to prayer. Prayer lifts itself up to God with all its strength, and begs for the treasure it longs for, which is the sweetness of contemplation. Contemplation when it comes rewards the labors of the other three; it inebriates the thirsting soul with the dew of heavenly sweetness. (Guigo, 1978, pp. 68, 79)

In monastic practice, Scriptures were read aloud at times set aside for reading and, for example, during meals. In the context of *lectio divina*, *meditatio* (meditation) consisted of an intellectual exercise of thinking about the text, for example, in an exegetical manner. It was a pondering of the text qua text. It could in principle be performed by an atheist or agnostic much as it would be performed by a monk. Guigo (1978) wrote: "The good and the wicked alike can read and meditate; and even pagan philosophers by the use of reason discovered the highest and truest good" (p. 72). *Oratio* (prayer), the third of the four procedures, turned *lectio divina* into a technique of Christian spirituality. An individual would turn toward God in prayer, seeking divine guidance in the personal application of the word, sentence, or brief passage that had been read and meditated. *Contemplatio* (contemplation) was the name given to guidance that came subsequently by spontaneous inspiration, as it were, out of nowhere. Contemplation was considered a gift of divine grace. Its occurrence was not predictable. It might not occur, or through grace it might occur very quickly. Referring presumably to his own experience, Guigo (1978) stated:

But the Lord, whose eyes are upon the just and whose ears can catch not only the words, but the very meaning of their prayers, does not wait until the longing soul has said all its say, but breaks in upon the middle of its prayer, runs to meet it in all haste, sprinkled with sweet heavenly dew, anointed with the most precious perfumes, and He restores the weary soul, He slakes its thirst, He feeds its hunger, He makes the soul forget all earthly things: by making it die to itself He gives it new life in a wonderful way, and by making it drunk He brings it back to its true senses. (pp. 73–74)

The final clauses possibly referred obliquely to meditations on the passion: "by making it die to itself He gives it new life in a wonderful way, and by making it drunk He brings it back to its true senses" (p. 74). The soul's death to itself was likened to drunkenness.

Guigo's meditations on the passion provide further and more explicit understanding of his spiritual experiences:

'All who belong to Christ, crucify their flesh.' But this is not enough; pagans have done this, and men 'greedy for worthless reputation' and hypocrites do it. They crucify their flesh, but they receive no reward from Christ. And this is because they have not the fear of God. Chasten my flesh with fear of you. Many have crucified their flesh, not for fear of you, but out of vainglory. This is not enough, then. Chasten with your fear the lechery not only of the body but also of the soul. Vainglory is the lechery of the soul. 'You destroy all those who have left you and gone whoring.' What does it matter whether the impurity of the flesh or the lechery of the soul is the cause of our destruction? And so we must carry a cross, which will crucify not only our flesh but our soul as well. The cross of the flesh is our body's mortification. The cross of the soul is the fear of God. The fear of God chastens the soul, so that it does not stray to right or left.

There is a third cross of the spirit, which is love. The Apostle says, 'I am nailed with Christ to the Cross: who will separate me from the love of Christ?' This was why the blessed Andrew would not be taken down from his cross. This cross is the love that gives us a heart of flesh, a soft and tender heart. So we see that this most gentle victim, Christ, was crucified because of His great love. Therefore, whoever attains to this third cross passes through the cloud between him and God and pours out his prayer in His very presence. (pp. 100–101)

Crucifixion with Christ generally referred to restriction of the passions through scrupulous moral behavior, asceticism, mortification of the flesh, and the aspiration to an emotional equanimity, *apatheia*. For Guigo, this order of crucifixion pertained to the flesh. It was preliminary to both crucifixion of the soul, which consisted of the fear of God, and crucifixion of the spirit, which consisted of the love of God. A person who "attains to this third cross . . . pours out his prayer in His very presence," engaging in *oratio* and receiving *contemplatio* in reply:

> Let the first cross, then, crucify the flesh through fear and reverence and knowledge, so that lechery may be chastised by fear, arrogance by reverence, excess by knowledge. Let the second cross win for the soul fortitude, counsel and understanding, so that by fortitude it may terrify the devil, and guide by counsel its neighbor, by understanding itself. The third cross transcends all this, and gathered into the unity of love may sleep in true peace and take its rest. (p. 101)

We may assume that Guigo arrived at his concept of three crucifixions through *lectio divina*. Elsewhere Guigo offered the novel idea that the thief who was crucified beside Christ was his most complete follower.

> First, imitation proceeds from love; for who is there who would not wish to imitate what he loves? Unless you love Christ you will not imitate Him, that is, you will not follow Him. For He said to Simon Peter after He had tested his love: 'Follow me', that is, 'Imitate me'. The feet of Judas may have followed Christ, but what his heart followed was avarice; and Gehazi followed Elisha not out of love but cupidity. But Christ must be followed with the love of our whole heart. So Meribbaal did not follow King David in time of trial, because he was lame: yet Christ must be followed at all times, but most of all when we are afflicted, because it is in difficulties that a friend is tested. Christ says: 'Whoever does not carry his cross and follow after me is not worthy of me.' Simon of Cyrene indeed carried the cross and followed Christ, but he did not share in the torments of the cross. We must follow Christ and we must cling to Him, and we must not desert Him until death. 'As the Lord lives', Scripture says, 'and your soul lives, I shall not leave you'; and Elisha never left his master until he was carried up in a chariot of fire. There were seventy-two disciples who followed Christ, but when they had heard Him say what they could not understand, they turned back. At the time of His Passion Peter followed Him, but from afar, because he was to deny Him. There was only the thief who followed Him to death upon the cross. Should I say that it was the thief who followed Christ to the death of the cross, or Christ who followed the thief?

Truly, Christ followed the thief until the thief could flee no farther, and when the flight failed the thief, he followed Christ, and with Christ entered into Paradise. (pp. 122–23)

In this passage, we may observe Guigo's *meditatio*, the expansion of the particular biblical verse that was being read with other texts that shared its motif of following. Guigo mentioned Christ and Simon Peter; Christ and Judas; Elisha and Gehazi; Meribbaal and King David; Simon of Cyrene and Christ; Elisha and Elijah; Christ and the seventy-two; Christ and Peter; and Christ and the thief. The question in the second last sentence may have been Guigo's *oratio*: "Should I say that it was the thief who followed Christ to the death of the cross, or Christ who followed the thief?" The response in the last sentence of the citation used the biblical figure of the thief as a metaphor by which to discuss a monk who engaged in meditation on the passion. We may assume that Guigo's *oratio* attempted to understand the personal relevance of the story of the thief. The *contemplatio* that he received in response similarly pertained to Guigo himself. Rather than address a private concern, this particular *contemplatio* happened to explain a theological topic that was applicable to anyone who meditated on the passion. "Christ followed the thief" when God became man and subject to death. Upon his death, "the thief could flee no farther." The experiential movement from the fear of God to the love of God was not a human achievement, but a divine initiative, a gift of grace: "when the flight failed the thief, he followed Christ, and with Christ entered into Paradise."

Meditation on the passion was also linked with *lectio divina* in *The Mirror of St. Edmund*, written at the end his life by Edmund Rich (c. 1170-1240), after he fled the See of Canterbury and entered the monastery of Pontigny in France. The text is notable for its expansion of the use of the term *contemplatio*.

Know thou that there are three kinds of contemplation. The first is in creatures. The second is in Holy Scripture. The third is in God Himself, in His nature. Contemplation is nothing else but the sight of the goodness of God. (Rich, 1905, p. 13)

By the contemplation of creatures, Edmund referred to the traditional topic of the omnipresence of God in the world of nature (pp. 13–15). Contemplation of Scripture consisted of *lectio divina* (pp. 17–18). Contemplation of God Himself could be done in two manners: "without in His Manhood, and within in His Godhead" (p. 58). The contemplation of God in His spiritual essence was again a traditional topic of monastic meditation; but contemplation of the incarnation, ministry, and passion of Jesus was a high medieval innovation. In all of its contexts, Edmund used the term "contemplation" in a sense consistent with Guigo's use of the term in reference to *lectio divina*. In Edmund's formulation, both *lectio divina* and meditation on the incarnation, ministry, and passion were equal in status to the two traditional topics of monastic contemplation, the immanence and transcendence of God.

PSYCHOANALYTIC REFLECTIONS

Following the revival of interest in *lectio divina* after Vatican II, a number of practitioners have gained expertise and explained the procedures in manners addressed to modern readers (Hall 1988; Casey, 1996a, 1996b; de Verteuil, 1996; Bianchi, 1998; Magrassi, 1998; Pennington, 1998; Dumont, 1999). The habitual accompaniment of verbal reasoning with mental imaging, which was taken for granted in the middle ages, no longer forms part of the practice. When the versatile, creative, and brilliant rhetoric of medieval texts such as Bernard of Clairvaux's sermons *On the Song of Songs* is recognized as a product of *lectio divina*, there can be little doubt that the medieval practice, like its living descendant, resembled free association as performed by psychoanalytic patients. The devotional and psychoanalytic procedures differ primarily in the association of *lectio* to the biblical text, where free association associates to the analysand's autobiography. Both procedures involve the cultivation of a receptive mental state, an effort to maintain emotional engagement and avoid drifting off into intellectualization, a search for patterns of behavior both in oneself and in others in one's life, a hope to understand the behavior from a point of view that is more objective than is customary, a concern with self-knowledge, and enormous variation in the details by which these general goals may be met.

Paraphrasing Freud's goal of making the unconscious conscious, Hans Loewald (1988) described the therapeutic action of psychoanalytic psychotherapy as the integration of emotional experience with the verbal content of self-knowledge:

> I view words and sentences as symbolic expressions that in their genuine function conjure up or evoke persons, things, events, and relations between them, and this on multiple levels of meaning. Words have the potential of awakening memories and fantasies that bring back to life, more or less vividly, the persons or things they name, thus arousing the listener. In derivative forms of verbal language, used in daily life much of the time, this more genuine function, here called symbolic, is deeply hidden, as good as lost, not intended or heard as such; the merely ideational, cognitive content of what is said is what counts. We may formulate this by saying that the derivative function of language consists in words referring to their referents (persons,

things, etc.) by abstraction, so that the listener now can refer to the same abstract referent, a kind of code that has a life of its own. In psychotherapy we try to set off a movement in which that kind of code is deciphered, revealed as symbolic, that is, condensing multilayered meanings rather than abstracting from them. That words can have this symbolic, summoning function, in its pure form used in primitive magic, is related to their being bodily phenomena, uttered by the speaker's vocal organs and transmitted to the listener's body through space. . . . I suggest that in the psychotherapeutic "talking cure" words are meant to find their way to their hidden symbolic power, gradually and sometimes suddenly, and that verbal communication between patient and therapist, carried on at this highly developed symbolic level, itself evokes more concrete emotional and bodily levels of communication. But the intent is not to create a one-way street leading from an ideational-verbal level to what we think of as deeper levels; the aim is an optimal congruity and mutual enrichment of levels (I aim at something similar as I write these lines of words). Since human development to civilized adulthood, as we see it, in its predominant trends is marked by symbolic action and its verbal communication, it is the communicative expression of feelings and thoughts in words that is the preferred method for mutual understanding in psychotherapy. One might say that the patient can be influenced by his own words insofar as their symbolic power and multiple meanings are made manifest to him by the therapist's verbal responses. (pp. 53–54)

Loewald attributed the therapeutic power of psychoanalysis to its ability to connect patients' conscious ideas of themselves to their deepest levels of emotion, creativity, and authenticity. *Lectio divina* aims similarly to connect meditators' conscious knowledge of Scripture to the deepest levels of their personhood, including emotions, creativity, interpersonal conduct, and so forth. In both cases, the harmonization of thought and feeling, of values and desires, increases self-knowledge, reduces mental conflict, and promotes emotional well-being.

To the extent that *lectio divina* works with unconscious inspiration to achieve a therapeutic integration of the heart and the mind, we may grant validity to Casey's (1996a, pp. 9–10) assertion: "Reading the Scriptures is the opposite of self-programming or any other kind of brain washing. It is allowing God to speak to our hearts, minds, and consciences." *Lectio divina* can produce contemplative states with affinities to the reveries that psychoanalytic patients inculcate through free association. Like children's play and the reveries of artists, poets, and other creative individuals, meditative reveries may ordinarily be expected to be psychohygienic. They are consistent with healthy personality growth. However, they are not ordinarily therapeutic. *Lectio divina* cannot be made to account for the reforming in faith and feeling that Hilton documented. Meditative reveries can be consoling and supportive, but they do not promote the type of rapid and dramatic personality change at which the better contemporary psychotherapies aim. Were it otherwise, the monasteries would long ago have put psychotherapists out of business.

Moreover, just as free association does not guarantee an analysand's entrance into a reverie state, the practice of *lectio divina* does not guarantee the achievement of a psychohygienic contemplative state. D. W. Winnicott (1971) explained:

> Psychotherapy takes place in the overlap of two areas of playing, that of the patient and that of the therapist. Psychotherapy has to do with two people playing together. The corollary of this is that where playing is not possible then the work done by the therapist is directed towards bringing the patient from a state of not being able to play into a state of being able to play. (p. 44)

At its most wholesome, *lectio divina* is a kind of serious, adult play with the biblical text that uses creative exegesis to achieve deepened understanding of self and faith. Consider, for example, the approach of William Flete's *Remedies Against Temptation*, a mid-fourteenth century text, which advised: "Though you feel stirrings of despair, or of unkindly and irreverent thoughts, comfort you ever more in the goodness of God, and in the painful passion that his manhood suffered" (Flete, 1968, p. 235; my translation). Flete explained that temptations were a means not only to be tested, but also to be purified:

> Leo the pope says that it falls sometimes that good and righteous souls be stirred by the fiend, and sometime by stirring of complexion to anger, troubles, tarryings, and diseases of dread, that it seems to them that their life is torment, and their death ease, in so much that sometimes for disease they begin to despair both of their life of body and of their soul. And they suppose that they are forsaken of God, who assays and proves his chosen friends by temptations and angers. But these findings or violent tempting and anguish are but purgings and provings of the soul, for as I set and said at the beginning of this writing as the fire purges gold, and a knight also is proved good and hardy by battle, right so temptations and troubles prove and purify the righteous man. (Flete, 1968, p. 224; my translation)

Implicit in Flete's perspective was a capacity to play conceptually with the idea of suffering in perspective of the passion narrative. A person who was brought to despair was to regard suffering neither simply as suffering, nor as punishment of sin, but rather as an opportunity for improvement that God gives precisely to those whom he loves:

> The more that a man or woman is troubled with the fiend against their will, the more clean they are before God, and here we learn openly that God suffers not his servants to be tempted but for their best, be so that they shape him to withstand the fiend as God's darlings should do. (pp. 228–29; my translation)

Suffering was not to be allowed to undermine a healthy sense of agency and self-esteem:

> And while that you have always . . . a good will to do well, and be mispaid with all evil thoughts and stirrings that you feel, and would never feel nor do other than is the will of God, though such wicked thoughts and stirrings come into your heart, and by great violence of sharpness of trouble and disease you are inclined to the will of sensuality, yet do not do it, nor consent to it, but it is sensuality that does it in you, and your good will stands still in you unbroken, though the clouds of evil thoughts stop away your sight from the feeling of your good will. (p. 229; my translation)

By contrast, a practitioner of *lectio divina* who cannot play creatively with exegesis and is fixated on a traditional or personal exegesis, cannot use use *lectio* playfully nor accept novel insights nor derive the psychohygienic benefits of the meditation. Consider, in this context, the teachings of the *Ancrene Wisse*, an anonymous thirteenth century guide for anchoresses:

> Above all other thoughts, in all your sufferings always think deeply on God's sufferings, that the ruler of the world was willing to suffer such humiliations for his servants—insults, blows, spitting, blindfolding, crowning with thorns set on his head in such a way that the bloody streams trickled down and flowed down to the earth; his sweet body bound naked to the hard pillar and beaten so much that the precious blood ran down on all sides; the poisonous drink they gave him when he thirsted on the cross, their heads wagging at him when they shouted loudly in mockery, "Look here at the one who healed others! Look how he heals and helps himself now!" (Matthew 27:39, 42). . . . compare all your woe, sickness, and whatever else—injury by word or by deed, and everything anyone can suffer—to what he suffered, and you will easily see how little it amounts to, especially if you

think that he was entirely innocent and that he did not endure all this for himself, since he never sinned. If you suffer sorrow, you have deserved worse; and all that you suffer, all, is for yourself.

So now, go along the difficult and laborious road toward the great feast of heaven where your glad friend awaits your coming, more gladly that the worldly fools go along the green road toward the gallows and the death of hell. It is better to go sick to heaven than healthy to hell, to mirth in misery than to sorrow in comfort. (Savage & Watson, 1991, pp. 117–18)

There was nothing playful, creative, or psychohygienic in this meditation. Indeed, the anchoress recognized her morbidity and defended it, insisting, "It is better to go sick to heaven than healthy to hell." The meditation offered no respite from the guilt that inhibited her. "If you suffer sorrow, you have deserved worse."

Ancrene Wisse was addressed to women who lived as anchoresses. They were solitaries who practiced asceticism, to a large extent avoiding sleep, food, and drink, physical comfort, and communication with other people. They lived walled into cells that were built alongside churches for the purpose. They regarded voluntary incarceration as a living death, a crucifixion that they owed Jesus in return for their salvation through his passion (Savage & Watson, 1991, pp. 1–2, 15–16; see also Warren, 1985). The mass for the dead was sung over them during the ceremony of enclosure, when the door was sealed and their contact with the world reduced to a window that overlooked the churchyard (Innes-Parker, 1999, p. 50). Anchoresses' practice of meditation confirmed them in their beliefs. By focusing on the insignificance of their own suffering in comparison with the misery that Jesus underwent, they made themselves contemptuous of human suffering, and confirmed themselves in their surrender to self-abuses.

In a similar fashion, Marguerite Porete wrote:

I pondered how He who was God and man was shamefully despised on earth for my sake, and [I pondered] the great poverty in which He placed Himself for my sake and the cruel death He suffered for my sake. In these three facts and points are all his deeds contained without comprehension. O Truth, Way, and Life, how is one to ponder this about you? It is a greater thing to inflame our hearts in love for you. (Porete, 1993, p. 208)

Porete was a Beguine who preached a doctrine of personal annihilation in the ecstasy of divine love. Her meditation on the passion was consistent with her teaching. She began by reflecting that Jesus' suffering was shameful and cruel. Granted that Jesus suffered for the sake of humanity, why did he create the necessity of his own suffering? What sense did it make? The passion precluded comprehension. With her reasoning stymied, she reflected on her emotional experience. Meditation on the passion served to encourage her love for Jesus. Whether she was motivated by gratitude and shame, or by excitement at the intensity of Jesus' love, we cannot know. She had the strength of character to pursue an independent line of mystical theology, but her pursuit of originality until she was burned at the stake as a relapsed heretic, indicates that unconscious self-harm was as important for her as conscious asceticism was for anchorites.

Similar psychodynamics may be found in *Christ Crucified*, a meditation on the passion by an anonymous Benedictine solitary who lived alone on the island of Farne in the late fourteenth century. The monk valued meditation on the passion because "a mind free from anxiety is like a perpetual feast, and fear does not abide in the charity which grows out of frequent meditation on our Lord's passion" (Monk & Facre, 1961, p. 51). The price that he paid for relief from anxiety was considerable. Meditation on the passion involved an embrace of guilt: "When I ponder in my heart how much thou must have loved me, even before I was born, to choose to suffer death on the cross rather than to allow me to be separated from thee for ever, I see that complete self-surrender on my part is due to thee, and that thou hast deserved to be loved by me above all others in return" (p. 77). Having distressed himself with meditation on the passion, the monk of Farne found solace in his reflections on the resurrection. To his thought, the hypostatic union of man and God in the person of Christ proved that humanity—and the monk—was eligible for salvation:

> When I fix my inward gaze upon the circle of the divine life, and behold my own nature so united to God in personal union, that a man should think it not robbery to be equal with God, whose good pleasure it is to dwell in him bodily according to the whole fullness of the Godhead; when I see flesh and blood sitting upon the throne of the Trinity, how greatly do you think shall I then rejoice with him in his glory and exult in God my Jesus! (p. 34)

The monk eloquently articulated his ambivalence toward God: "Who would deny the sweetness of that love of Christ's humanity which can crucify man's flesh with its vices and concupiscences?" (p. 83). We may interpret the monk's embrace of the monastic ideal of apatheia as a compromise formation that permitted him to repress consciousness of his conflicted emotionality:

> The third [and final] degree is reached when a man is so fired with the love of God that he is neither elated by prosperity nor cast down

by adversity, and if riches abound, he by no means sets his heart on them; if he happens to lose them, it causes him no regret at all. This is the wisest and most perfect love of God and is itself proof that all worldly love is dead. For who can be wiser than the man who has lost all taste for this world and delights in the love of God alone. (p. 90)

For *Ancrene Wisse*, Marguerite Porete, and the Monk of Farne, meditation on the passion promoted an identification with Jesus' suffering that the writers internalized psychologically and enacted through their interpersonal behavior. We may assume that morbid trends in their personalities attracted them to the morbid interpretations that they placed on the passion; but we must also conclude that their meditations on the passion confirmed them in their neuroses, intensifying their psychopathologies by providing religious content for neurotic repetition-compulsions. The consolations that they found in religion included reinforcements of guilt, shame, obedience, and self-harm that they intensified through their meditations. In their use, meditation could be a religious means of obsessing over negativity.

In contrast with Freud's (1927, 1930) categorical rejection of religion as an illusion or, worse, a delusion, contemporary psychoanalysts tend increasingly to agree with the formulation of Oskar Pfister (1948), a Lutheran pastor who became a psychoanalyst and Freud's personal friend.

The neurosis of individuals leads to a neurotic malformation of their Christian faith, and in certain circumstances must do so inevitably; and when this process is applied to the masses it necessarily affects entire Churches. . . . Conversely a neurotic, perverted Christianity must induce neuroses in the individual and in the masses. (p. 24)

Individuals make use of religion in accordance with their personal circumstances: gender, age, physical and mental health, occupation, familial, economic, and social positions, and so forth. Out of all of a religious tradition's variant contents, individuals pick and choose the particular features that resonate with their own circumstances. Oversimplifying, we may say that neurotic individuals tend to make neurotic uses of religion, while more wholesome personalities use religion to more wholesome effects.

Consider, for example, the Christian doctrine of the crucifixion, that Jesus died to redeem humanity. Jesus' ability to remain loving while absorbing massive abuse replicates the posture of a mother—or a psychoanalyst—who permits aggression to manifest long enough that it can be resolved and outgrown (Suttie, 1935, p. 142; Hopkins, 1989). However, a person incapable of intimacy, incapable of receiving love, might find a threat of intimacy in Jesus' loving embrace, which is symbolized by his arms outstretched on the cross, and fear of Jesus' love may lead to an unconscious wish for his crucifixion (Meyerson & Stollar, 1962). The crucifixion is frequently experienced—as, for example, by solitaries—as the consummate act of a syndrome of voluntary emotional martyrdom that Fromm (1947, pp. 136–37) termed "neurotic unselfishness." The syndrome consists of overly helpful, unrequested, and ostensibly generous behavior that induces shame in its beneficiaries for their lesser achievements, inhibits their criticism, and generally demands their gratitude, admiration, and obedience. Neurotic unselfishness is a vehicle by which the powerless may wield power by manipulating others' capacities for shame, guilt, and anxiety. The neurotic unselfishness that is traditionally attributed to Jesus has often been used by the churches to demand masochistic surrenders to authoritarian teachings, texts, and persons. At the same time, resentment over indebtedness to Christ may compound guilt and lead to satisfaction—not sorrow—with Christ's function as a scapegoat (Flugel, 1945, p. 166). The unconscious resentment of Jesus, and guilt over the resentment, may also be displaced onto his coreligionists, the Jews, leading to anti-Semitism (Fenichel, 1940; Simmel, 1946; Tarachow, 1960). The health and morbidity of the doctrine of the crucifixion varies with the personalities that integrate the doctrine in their living religiosity (Forster & Carveth, 1999).

A psychoanalyst must always question with each patient what sort of spirituality is being allowed to manifest. In psychoanalysis, the aspirations to free association and analytic impartiality are intended to permit the unconscious to manifest as fully as it is able. *Lectio divina* differs significantly. The God that is allowed to speak through *lectio divina* is a God whose living word is censored by Scripture and ecclesiastic authority. In speaking through the passion and resurrection, God is further limited in what he may say. There is much that God might say, for example, to a Jew or a Muslim or a Hindu that the New Testament inhibits a Christian from hearing. If God speaks outside the assertions of authoritative texts, Christians are apt to disallow his words as the temptations of evil spirits. Cultural fixations, no differently than personal inhibitions, place pathological constraints on religion.

Although contemplative states can be used therapeutically, they do not ordinarily address established psychopathology. Unlike psychoanalysis, contemplation has never been suggested as a replacement for the practice of exorcism. In Christian practice, exorcism is ritual and performative. The ritual is conducted and the community behaves as though demons have been expelled. The transformation of the community's behavior provides the sufferer with a corresponding measure of relief from interpersonal distress, but personality disturbances remain unaddressed. As therapy, exorcism involves more than a placebo effect. Exorcism is genuinely supportive therapy, but it promotes neither insight nor therapeutic personality change.

Chapter 4

Mystical Death

Hilton (1983) listed "praying, reading Holy Scripture [and] meditating on the passion of Christ" (p. 18) as his principle means of devotion. His phrasing indicates a distinction in his mind between *lectio divina* and meditation on the passion. Hilton's concept is consistent, I suggest, with an interpretation of meditation on the passion that the Swedish historian of religion Geo Widengren advanced in a little noted article entitled "Researches in Syrian mysticism" (1961). In the course of a discussion of the impact of Origenism on an ascetic-mystical movement in Syriac Christianity in the sixth through ninth centuries, Widengren argued for a phenomenological resemblance among the visions of the passion that were cultivated by the Syriac mystics, the fourteenth-century Dominican Henry Suso, and in *The Spiritual Exercises* of St. Ignatius of Loyola.

> If we compare these methods with those used by the Syrian monks we find the resemblance are [sic] great. . . . We find exactly the same psychological laws . . . we have come across a definite psychological method of prayer with an able guidance of the monk, making him pass through several stages until he reaches the last, "the pure prayer", the ecstatic experience. (Widengren, 1961, pp. 180–81)

Widengren characterized the "inner vision" that the mystics attained as an "experience of mystical death" (p. 180), a discrete variety of mystical experience that students of comparative religion also term "ecstatic" and "initiatory death" (Corbin, 1954, pp. 156–57; 1971, p. 79; Eliade, 1958). Mystical death closely resembles a panic attack in consisting of an urgent conviction of immediately impending death that is often accompanied by intense fear and vivid visual

47

imaginations of dying. Unlike panic attacks, however, mystical deaths tend to resolve spontaneously through the realization that the experience of dying is an imagination, and repeated experience of mystical death can lead to equanimity at their onset. Mystical deaths may be followed immediately by mystical unions, possibly indicating that the panic states are products of resistance to unitive ideas that are pressing for admission to consciousness (Merkur, 1999, pp. 87–93). Because some of Widengren's historical assumptions and much of his psychological commentary reflect the scholarship of an older era, the enduring force of his observations is best presented through a fresh review of the data.

THE SYRIAC MYSTERY OF THE CROSS

Meditation on the passion of Jesus was discussed in a series of sixth- and seventh-century documents of the Syriac Church. The most famous Syriac-speaking churchmen, such as pseudo-Macarius, Ephrem the Syrian, and pseudo-Dionysius the Areopagite, wrote in Greek in order to reach an international audience. The texts that discussed meditation on the passion were instead written in Syriac, which is a dialect of ancient Aramaic and is written in an alphabet of its own. In the Syriac Church, mystics cultivated experiences of mystical death through visionary practices that they termed "the mystery of the cross" (Widengren, 1961). Monks visualized themselves as Christ crucified. Joseph Hazzaya (1934, p. 182) wrote: "Continual prayer is the perfection of all the commandments, and the intelligible Cross of which our Lord said that anyone who takes it up and follows Him will inherit eternal life with Him." Isaac of Nineveh (1923, p. 150) stated: "Thou . . . who art victorious, taste the suffering of Christ in thy person, that thou also mayest be deemed worthy of tasting His glory. For if we suffer with Him, we shall also be glorified with Him." He also wrote: "I gaze at Thee by the compulsion of the bonds of the cross . . . which is the crucifixion of the mind" (p. 151). In his vision, a monk was to experience himself as Jesus, dying and resurrecting.

Dadisho Katraya specified that a monk was to visualize a good angel to his right, and an evil angel or demon to his left. Presumably the angel and demon were visualized as being crucified on crosses to the left and right of the cross on which Jesus was hanged. Katraya (1934) wrote:

> Look also in your mind at the angel who is at your right hand and at the demon who is standing at your left hand, and so think spiritually of the meaning of every word that comes out of your mouth, and do not allow distraction to prevail upon you. (pp. 139–40)

In order to produce a sense of identification with Jesus, the monk was to move rapidly in his thoughts between Jesus and himself. He was also to maintain the visualization of the two angels.

> In reciting the Psalm: "O God, deliver me out of the hand of the wicked and out of the hand of the unrighteous and cruel man," when you say "O God," look towards our Lord on the Cross; when you say "deliver me" look at yourself and towards the holy angel who is standing at your right hand, and through whom you are being delivered; and when you say "out of the hand of the wicked and of the unrighteous and cruel man," look in your thought at the wicked demon who is standing at your left hand and who hates you and fights against you. Furthermore, when you recite "Let them be ashamed and brought to confusion together that rejoice at mine hurt, and let them be clothed with shame that magnify themselves against me," turn your sight towards the demon. (p. 140)

As the monk's prayers continued, he could expect his active efforts of visualization to be rewarded by the onset of imagery in which various events would occur spontaneously. However, the image of Jesus crucified was to be maintained actively:

> When you recite "Let them shout for joy and be glad that favour my victory" look in your thought at the holy angel who helps you, and at his holy brother-angels who often repair to him in order to honour him and to express their joy in your exercises. And when you recite "Let them say continually that the Lord is great who had pleasure in the peace of His servant," look also in your mind at our Lord on the Cross. (p. 140)

Visualization of demons formed an integral part of the meditations. Terror and fright occurred frequently during the visualizations and were attributed to the demons. Faith in Jesus would suffice, however, to cause the fear to subside. Joy would then follow:

> And when you recite "Let the demons be cursed, but mayest Thou, O Lord, be blessed, and may I, Thy servant, rejoice in Thee," in saying "Let them be cursed" look at the demons; in saying "mayest Thou be blessed" look at our Lord; and in saying "Thy servant" think of yourself and of your angel. And if the demon waxes wrathful and terrifies you with his visions and frightens you with his temptations, be not afraid, excited and disturbed, but look at our Lord on the Cross, and

have trust and confidence in the holy angel who is standing at your right hand to help you and guard you. In this way your fear will immediately vanish and you will be filled with joy. Act in this way when you pray at the end of each Doxology. (p. 140)

The meditation culminated in a joy whose intensity "has no parallel in creation." The euphoria coincided with intellectual illuminations whose contents presumably varied from person to person.

And during your prayer and your recitation of the Psalms, your intelligence will be illuminated with understanding and strengthened by hope, and will shed sweet tears mingled with joy and love. At the end of your service you will rejoice in God with a joy that has no parallel in creation, like a man possessing the treasure of life in his soul, and through your joy, in your vigils, your recitation of the Psalms and your prayer, the labour of the canonical Hours of the day will be lightened for you. In this way, through the continual and daily labours which you experience in your solitude, you will dwell in the mighty refuge of Christ, which leads to the House of God. (p. 141)

The Syriac mystery of the cross used mental images to induce visionary experiences in which the visionaries saw themselves as Jesus in the act of dying on the cross. The desired experience was a mystical death that often involved terror and fright at the prospect of dying immediately.

THE BLESSED HENRY SUSO

Heinrich von Berg was born around 1300 in Constance or perhaps the neighboring town of Überlingen. His mother's maiden name was Süs or Süse. Following her death, Heinrich took her surname to perpetuate her memory. Known in English as Henry Suso, Heinrich Süse entered the Dominican friary of Constance as a novice at the age of thirteen. Initially casual in his observance of the Rule, at eighteen Suso became severe with himself. He engaged in austerities, mortification, and seclusion for several years, and he was then sent to Cologne to complete his studies at the *studium generale* of the Order. Meister Eckhart was a lector at Cologne during the same period. It is not known whether Suso was Eckhart's student prior to his trial and condemnation in 1328, but Suso knew and defended Eckhart's teachings in his own writings. Suso did not proceed to Paris to become a *magister*, but instead returned to Constance, where he taught in the friary school. After several years in the office of lector, he was elected prior. In 1339, when most of the Dominicans in

Constance supported the Pope against the Emperor, they were banished for ten years. In his autobiography, *The Life of the Servant*, Suso wrote of his exile as a turning point in his life. He abandoned asceticism, mortification, seclusion, teaching, and writing. He turned instead to preaching and pastoral care at Dominican convents, Beguine houses, and elsewhere in the vicinity of Constance. He became one of the leaders of the "Friends of God." However, a woman accused him of fathering her illegitimate child. The scandal was probably responsible for Suso's move to Ulm around 1348. He lived there until his death on January 25, 1366 (Clark, 1949, pp. 55–60).

Among the many and varied spiritual practices and contemplations that Suso described in his writings, he discussed his manner of meditation on the passion:

> The first step was that every night after matins in his customary place—the chapter room—conforming himself to Christ, he would devote himself to feeling sympathy for everything his Lord and God, Christ, had suffered before him. He arose and went from corner to corner to shake off all laziness and to remain wide awake in feeling the suffering. He began by joining with Christ at the Last Supper and suffering together with him from place to place until he accompanied him to Pilate. Finally, he took his condemned Lord to his trial and went with him then the lonely way of the cross from the place of judgment all the way to under the cross.
>
> His way of the cross was as follows: When he came to the doorstep of the chapter room, he knelt down and kissed the first footsteps Christ made when, already condemned, he turned and was about to go to his death. He began to recite the psalm of our Lord's suffering: "*Deus, deus meus, respice me.*" And then he went through the door and into the cloisters. There were four paths on which he accompanied him to his death.
>
> He accompanied him on the first path to death through a desire to abandon both friends and transitory goods, and to suffer hopeless abandonment and voluntary poverty in praise of him.
>
> On the second path he resolved to reject transitory honor and dignity, to be despised willingly by this whole world, realizing that Christ had become a worm and was scorned by all men.
>
> At the beginning of the third path he knelt down again and kissed the ground to symbolize a voluntary surrender of all unnecessary comfort and pampering of the body, to the great pain of his soft body, and he imagined, as it is written there, how Christ's strength dried up and his nature died away. And as they drove Christ forward so woefully, he called to mind how right it was for all eyes to grow damp and for all hearts to sigh.

When he came to the fourth path, he knelt down in the middle as though he were kneeling in front of the gate through which Christ would have to go out. Falling down in front of him, he kissed the ground, calling upon him and asking him not to go to his death without him, and that he let him go along because he had a right to go along. He imagined all this to himself as vividly as he could, and he spoke the prayer "*Ave rex noster, fili David,*" etc. and let Christ lead the way.

After this he knelt down a second time facing the gate and received the cross with the verse: "*O crux ave, spes unica,*" and let it pass by. Then he knelt down facing the gentle Mother, who in her immeasurable grief was led past him. He noticed how distressed she was—the hot tears, the plaintive sighs, the sorrowful demeanor. He remembered her with a "*Salve Regina*" and kissed her footsteps.

Then he got up quickly and strode after his Lord to catch up to him. His imagining was sometimes very vivid, just as if he were really walking at his side. He recalled how, when King David was banished from his kingdom, his most gallant knights rallied around him and loyally came to his aid. Then he surrendered his will. Whatever God did with him, for the sake of Christ let it always be. Finally he took up the epistle from the prophet Isaiah that is read during holy week, which reads, "*Domine, quis credidit auditu nostro,*" which clearly portrays his being led out to his death. Then he went to the door of the choir and climbed up the stairs to the pulpit. When he came beneath the cross, where he had once experienced the hundred thoughts on the passion, he knelt to watch his Lord being stripped of his clothing and nailed to the cross. Then he took the discipline and with heartfelt agony nailed himself on the cross with his Lord, begging him that neither life nor death, joy nor sorrow be able to separate his servant from him. (Suso, 1989, pp. 84–85)

In meditating on Christ's passion, Suso's practice was to "devote himself to feeling sympathy for everything his Lord God, Christ, had suffered before him." For example, "he imagined, as it is written there, how Christ's strength dried up and his nature died away. And as they drove Christ forward so woefully, he called to mind how right it was for all eyes to grow damp and for all hearts to sigh." At another point in the procession, Suso stated that "falling down in front of him, he kissed the ground, calling upon him and asking him not to go to his death without him, and . . . he let him go along because he had a right to go along. He imagined all this to himself as vividly as he could." Suso found that his exercises of vivid imagination induced visions. "His imagining was sometimes very vivid, just as if he were really walking at his side." At the climax of the passion, Suso experienced crucifixion with Christ. "Then he took the discipline and with heartfelt agony nailed himself on the cross with his Lord, begging him that neither life nor death, joy nor sorrow be able to separate his servant from him."

Suso also remarked that "he had another interior way of making the way of the cross." In this second technique, he commiserated with Mary (Suso, 1989, p. 85) and did not identify with Jesus. Suso was conscious of the phenomenological distinction between his visualizations of his own death and the Anselmian tradition that meditated on the passion from the imagined perspective of an eyewitness.

The extraordinary character of Suso's visions has provoked repeated discussion from psychological perspectives (Delacroix, 1908, pp. 308–24; Leuba, 1925, pp. 60–65; Lindblom, 1962, pp. 42–43; Widengren, 1961; Arbman, 1963, pp. 58–75). What began as deliberate imaginings ended in pseudohallucinatory experiences. They had the vividness of hallucinations, but they were known to be such at the time of their experience. There was, however, no apparent loss of sense perception, nor any other evidence of a state of trance, dissociation, or fugue. Visualization yielded to pseudohallucination, and the pseudohallucination consisted of Suso's mystical death.

IGNATIAN SPIRITUALITY

Perhaps the most famous discussion of mental imaging in Latin Christianity occurs in *The Spiritual Exercises* of St. Ignatius of Loyola (1491–1556). Ignatius designed a series of meditations that were to be performed over a four-week period. Each meditation was devoted to a specific mental image for a period of one hour. Different meditations were to be performed during the course of each day. The first week was devoted to meditations on sin and hell; the second week to the birth and infancy of Jesus. Individual portions of the passion narrative occupied the first six days of the third week of the *Exercises*. Exercitants meditated on "the whole Passion at once" on the last day of the third week.

Ignatius discussed the passion in the course of a general introduction to mental imaging.

> *Preparatory prayer.* Ask our Lord God for the grace to direct my thoughts, activities and deeds in the service and praise of His Divine Majesty.
> *First preliminary.* An imaginative representation of the place.
> *Note.* For a visual contemplation or meditation, the picture is an imaginative representation of the physical place where the event to be contemplated occurs. . . .

Second Preliminary. I ask our Lord God for what I want. This prayer must be appropriate to the subject-matter. If I am contemplating the Resurrection, I will pray for a share in Christ's joy; if the Passion, I will ask for suffering, grief and agony, in the company of Christ in agony. (Ignatius, 1963, pp. 30–31)

In Ignatius' instructions, we may recognize both the *meditatio* and the *oratio* of *lectio divina*. The grace that he sought differed, however, from the *contemplatio* of *lectio divina*. Ignatius sought the occurrence of an emotion. "This is the gift proper to the Passion—sorrow in company with Christ in His sorrow, being crushed with the pain that crushed Christ, tears and a deepfelt sense of suffering, because Christ suffered so much for me" (Ignatius, 1963, p. 69). There was no prayer for an intellectual apprehension that might be received as a personal revelation in a dialogue or conversation with God. There was prayer only for an appropriate emotional response to the meditations. For Ignatius, the occurrence of an emotion in response to a meditation was a gift of grace. It was a kind of *contemplatio* whose revelation of a particular emotion implied the attitude and will of God. Ignatius discussed the drawing of inferences from emotional occurrences during meditation as a discernment of spirits. In his view, emotional responses to meditation were necessary in order to know and be able to conform with the will of God. The *Spiritual Exercises* were designed for the express purpose of inculcating a capacity, by means of emotional states, simultaneously to know and to want what God wants (Newman, 1996, pp. 52–53; Meissner, 1999, pp. 205, 227). Meditation on the passion during the third week of the *Exercises* serves, for example, to educate the exercitant's appreciation of human suffering.

> Christ's suffering becomes our own, and only through union with his suffering does love deliver us from evil and make our suffering redemptive. The election itself involves a conversion, a turning from sin to grace, from self-absorption to love, from sinfulness to forgiveness. (Meissner, 1999, p. 228)

Empathy with the passion remains part of the living practice of Ignatian spirituality (Meissner, 1999, p. 226). The pastoral psychologist Paul Pruyser (1976) stated:

> In certain phases of the systematic "meditations," as they are called, the retreat master urges the retreatant to imagine as vividly as possible the excruciating sufferings of Jesus at the various stages of the cross, to identify himself with the agonies of his Lord to the point of sweating, signing, or moaning, and to "live" for a time in these almost hallucinatory stages. (p. 71)

Ignatius devoted the first day of the fourth week of his *Exercises* to the resurrection. The meditations again involved mental images of events that were narrated in the gospels (Ignatius, 1963, p. 76). For his meditations on the life of Jesus, Ignatius was indebted to Ludolf of Saxony's *Vita Jesu Christi*, which he read at the time of his conversion; Ludolf's text had drawn on the *Meditationes vitae Christi* (Ragusa, 1961), a late thirteenth- or early fourteenth-century text that was popularly but wrongly attributed to St. Bonaventure.

After a corporeal resurrection had been imagined in close detail, Ignatius had his exercitants cultivate a purely intellectual experience that was immersed in the world of sense perceptions. In his "Contemplation for Achieving Love," Ignatius (1963) wrote:

> Think of God energizing, as though He were actually at work, in every created reality, in the sky, in matter, plants and fruits, herds and the like: it is He who creates them and keeps them in being, He who confers life or consciousness, and so on. (p. 80)

God's presence in creation had been a traditional topic of contemplation from the Desert Fathers onward. Ignatius was more immediately indebted to Garcia Jimenez de Cisneros's *Book of Exercises for the Spiritual Life* (1500) which his confessor at Montserrat had given to him (Meissner, 1999, p. 102). As the climactic, unitive way of his program, de Cisneros (1929) had devoted a week of meditations to teleological considerations of the perceptible world (pp. 145–46,150–51,154–55).

A CISTERCIAN AND FRANCISCAN PRACTICE

Widengren was correct, I suggest, in noticing that deliberate efforts to visualize the passion of Jesus led to visionary states in early medieval Syrian mysticism, the late medieval practice of Henry Suso, and Ignatian spirituality, which dates to the Counter-Reformation. Mystical deaths were common to the Syrians and Suso, as we have seen; but Ignatian spirituality preserves the perspective of an eyewitness of the passion. For present purposes, however, it is most important that James of Milan and Walter Hilton both referred unmistakably to mystical death. James of Milan specified that a meditator was to "be as he were turned into God" before he thought "points of Christ's passion" (Hilton, 1952, pp. 139–40). Having visualized himself as God, the meditator would implicitly experience Christ's crucifixion as his own mystical death. Citing Matthew 16:24, "If anyone wants to be a follower of mine, let him renounce himself and take up his cross and follow me," Hilton (1991, p. 113) similarly instructed meditators to visualize crucifixion in their imaginations: "take cross . . . and then follow (that is to say, into contemplation)." which implies that taking the cross was to be done in meditation. Elsewhere Hilton (1991) wrote of the image of God that is the human soul:

> What are you to do with this image? I answer you with the word that the Jews spoke to Pilate about Christ: *Tolle, Tolle, crucifige eum!* [John 19:15: Take him away! Take him away! Crucify him!] Take this body of sin and put it upon the cross. That is to say, Break down this image and slay the false love of sin in yourself. (p. 156)

Hilton's language was not metaphoric. He referred literally to a mental image of the meditator's body whose crucifixion was to be visualized.

Medieval references to mystical death through meditation on the passion are rare, but they suffice to locate Suso, James of Milan, and Walter Hilton as heirs to a venerable tradition of Cistercian and Franciscan meditation. St. Bernard of Clairvaux (1090–1153), the most influential mystical theologian of the twelfth century, encouraged meditation on the passion in Sermons 20 and 43 of his sermons *On the Song of Songs* (Bernard, 1971, pp. 152; 1976, pp. 221–23). Unlike Syriac writers, Latin writers rarely referred to terror and fright at the climax of their meditations on the passion. Their writings led readers to anticipate grief, pain, and sorrow, but also an equanimity and acceptance. Bernard (1976) remarked, for example, that meditation on the passion led sometimes to "a drink that is wholesomely bitter, sometimes an unction that is sweet and consoling" (p. 222). Not every effort to meditate on the passion led to an experience that was deeply distressing. Fear and terror might occur, however. Writing in his third series of *Sentences*, Bernard specified that Christ's subjective experience had included fear and terror:

> Christ experienced fear, for as we read in the Gospel: 'He began to be afraid and distressed'. But he felt this fear willingly, rather than because of his condition. He felt sorrow because he chose to, not because as a Jew he was able to do so. Thus it is written: 'My soul is sad, even unto death'. In this fear of Christ we should take note of three things: the will of the Father, the desire of Christ's spirit, and the inclination of his flesh. The will of the Father was to complete the work of redemption, and specifically to redeem the human race through Christ's death. The desire of Christ's spirit was to obey the Father. The inclination of his flesh, however, was to avoid death, since it is natural for the flesh to be terrified of death. The will of the Father was honored, the desire of the spirit crowned, and inclination of the flesh properly controlled. So although Christ said: 'Father, if it is pos-

sible, let this cup pass from me,' he immediately added: 'but let it be not as I wish, but as you will.' (Bernard, 2000, p. 384)

Since the passion had involved fear and terror that were attributable to the humanity of Jesus, Bernard implied that any human being who meditated on the passion might similarly experience fear and terror at the prospect of death.

In another passage in the same text, Bernard referred explicitly to dying with Christ while meditating on the passion:

> The recollection and emulation of the death of Jesus Christ are the waters of Siloam, in which we can wash and be cleansed of our sins. From these two derive the charisms of grace, the waters of paradise, the draughts of tears, the gifts of charity, the inducements to virtue, true means of consolation, the remedies provided by God. . . . We ought to suffer with him who suffered, be crucified with him who was crucified, and die along with him who died by remembering this lovingly and imitating it devoutly; if we wish to reign in glory with him; for the joy of ruling comes only after a time of pain. One reaches the glory of majesty through the cup of suffering, and no one can achieve that through which he will possess eternal bliss, unless he first drinks of that whereby he will endure temporal grief. (Bernard, 2000, pp. 398–99)

"Recollection and emulation," like "remembering . . . and imitating," referred to identifying with Jesus while meditating on his passion. The meditations were not to be limited to suffering and being crucified, but to include dying "along with him who died."

Bernard's friend and fellow Cistercian, William of St. Thierry (c. 1085–1148), referred briefly to mystical death at the end of an extensive discussion of meditation on the passion:

> 6. For the effect of our redemption is repeated in us as often as we recall it in affective prayer. . . . with even greater daring we make a mental picture of your passion for ourselves, so that our bodily eyes may possess something on which to gaze, something to which to cleave, worshipping not the pictured likeness only, but the truth the picture of your passion represents.
> 7. For when we look more closely at the picture of your passion, although it does not speak, we seem to hear you say: "When I loved you, I loved you to the end. Let death and hell lay hold on me, that I may die their death; eat, friends, and drink abundantly, beloved, unto life eternal." And in this way your cross becomes to us like the linen

sheet that was shown to blessed Peter, let down from heaven by four corners. All sorts went into it, clean creatures and unclean; and we rejoice that we are lifted up to heaven, where also we, who were unclean, are cleansed.

For through this picturing of your Passion, O Christ, our pondering on the good that you have wrought for us leads us forthwith to love the highest good. . . . he who enters by you, O Door, walks on the smooth ground and comes to the Father, to whom no one may come, except by you. And he no longer labors to understand knowledge beyond his reach, for the bliss of a well-disposed conscience absorbs him utterly. And as the river of joy floods that soul more completely, she seems to see you as you are. In sweet meditation on the wonderful sacrament of your passion. . . . She seems to herself to see you face to face, when you thus show her, in the cross and in the work of your salvation, the face of the ultimate Good. The cross itself becomes for her the face of a mind that is well-disposed toward God. (William, 1970, pp. 153–54)

The mechanics of the meditative process were mentioned in the first paragraph. A meditator was to begin by entertaining a mental image. "We make a mental picture of Thy Passion for ourselves." Later, however, this mental image became the vehicle of divine grace, through which a revelation was disclosed. "Your cross becomes to us like the linen sheet that was shown to blessed Peter, let down from heaven by four corners." Through this transformation of a deliberate effort at visualization into a heaven-sent vision, access was gained to religious experiences more generally. "We rejoice that we are lifted up to heaven, where also we, who were unclean, are cleansed." Meditation on the passion provided access to "the face of the Supreme Good," the Father.

William asserted that meditation on the passion results in a distinctive religious experience. "He who enters by you, O Door. . . . no longer labors to understand knowledge beyond his reach, for the bliss of a well-disposed conscience absorbs him utterly." William described a euphoric experience: "the river of joy floods that soul." The cognitive content of the experience was an apprehension of God: the soul "seems to see you as you are."

The final clause of this passage reverted to the idea that crucifixion was experienced as one's own and was not merely imagined as from the perspective of an onlooker. "The cross itself becomes for her," meaning the meditator's soul, "the face of the mind that is well-disposed to God," that is, the face of the meditator. Put more simply, the soul finds her own face as the face of the person crucified on the cross.

Aelred of Rievaulx (1110–1167), a Cistercian abbot in Yorkshire, discussed meditation on the passion from the perspective of an eyewitness in a treatise, titled *A Rule of Life for a Recluse*, that he addressed to his sister (Aelred, 1971, pp. 89–90). A single statement earlier in the treatise indicates that the passion was not only to be witnessed, but was instead to be imitated. Referring to the furnishings of a recluse's oratory, Aelred recommended: "On your altar let it be enough for you to have a representation of our Savior hanging on the Cross; that will bring before your mind his Passion for you to imitate" (Aelred, 1971, p. 73). The phrasing does not permit decision whether Aelred meant that a recluse was to be crucified in a metaphoric sense, or in the mental images that we would expect of a Cistercian of his period. Only slightly less equivocation may be found in a sermon for the feast of Easter (Aelred, 1971). In a passage commencing, "What could the remembrance of the Lord's passion effect in your hearts?" (p. 187), Aelred initially adopted the perspective of an eyewitness:

> *He humbled himself, becoming obedient unto death, even the death on the cross.* Look at the degradation. But listen to what comes next. *Therefore God exalted him.* . . . His suffering were soon finished, his death was soon transformed. . . .
>
> Now, what sweetness was your heart able to imbibe when, with your inner eye, you saw the Lord carrying his cross? Who can appreciate that humility, that meekness, that patient endurance? . . . How sweet it was to reflect on the, as it were, still fresh wounds of Christ, to stand as it were by his cross, to see the tears of his mother, to hear that sweet voice [say]: *Father, forgive them for they know not what they do.* What hope for the forgiveness of our sins does not surge up in us when we hear him praying so sweetly even for his enemies. (pp. 188–89)

At this point in the meditation, Aelred shifted perspective and enjoined meditators to adopt Jesus' emotions as their own:

> But this sweetness was not that of milk but that of wine. For while on the one hand it tasted sweet, on the other it had a bite. The sweetness lay in affection and devotion but at the same time a certain tender sadness and compassion gave it that bite. You should not be able to look at those sweet hands being pierced with nails so hard without sadness, albeit sweet. . . Therefore, you who have tasted this biting wine—that is, the remembrance of the Lord's passion—now crave milk—that is, the gentleness of his resurrection. And it is rightly milk, for there is no sadness mixed in with it. (pp. 188–90)

The sermon continued with discussions of other matters, but it returned to the topic of meditation on the passion in its final paragraph.

Aelred's sermon concluded with an explicit claim that meditation on both the passion and the resurrection proceeded from the perspective of Jesus: "Once we have put off the old man who we had been, who was crucified with Christ, as Christ has risen from the dead through the Glory of the Father, may we, having been crucified with him and buried to all the desires of this world, deserve to rise to a new life. And in the future resurrection may we deserve to rejoice with him for ever" (p. 193).

A century later, Stephen of Sawley (d. 1252), a Cistercian abbot in Northumberland, discussed meditations on the passion with greater candor. Stephen recommended the perspective of an eyewitness in a treatise entitled *Meditations*. In *A Mirror for Novices*, the meditator was instead to adopt Jesus' point of view. The crucifixion was initially to be experienced from the perspective of an eyewitness, but at its climax, the meditator was to experience Jesus' death as his own:

> Recall his Passion in like manner: the derision, spitting, cuffing, chaining of his hands, blindfolding, the scourging ordered by Pilate, the mockery of Herod, the jeering voices which demanded his crucifixion and the mocking soldiers intoxicated with sour wine who genuflected before him and hit him on the head with rods. See him on the cross, his hands elevated 'like the evening sacrifice'—his limbs stretched, his face pale, his bones in pain, his joints broken—and his great bitterness which finally brought on the separation of his soul and spirit.
>
> I firmly believe that, if you diligently cultivate these or similar thoughts as time permits, you will find a sea 'great and wide.'
>
> Picture Jesus on the cross, heaped with reproaches and derision, his body completely lacerated, his flesh torn by whips and thorns as he hung nailed to the cross. Visualize him as he directs his merciful and loving eyes on you, the son of perdition. Filled with grief, cast aside your ingratitude and rebuke your hardness of heart.
>
> Realize who is suffering. See what he is going through and for whom, how dearly he has purchased your love, how willingly he gave himself for you; there the weakness of hanging there will be yours, the pallor of shaking limbs yours, the shedding of blood yours, and the last breath of the crucified yours. (pp. 97–98)

Identification with Jesus was to occur during the climactic visualization of the crucifixion: "the weakness of hanging there will be yours, the pallor of shaking limbs yours, the shedding of blood yours, and the last breath of the crucified yours." Equally explicit identification with Jesus was to be made when meditating on his ascension. Here again the meditations were to commence with the perspective of an eyewitness, but the experience was to culminate in union and oneness with God:

> Recalling his ascension, be mindful of the following: if you hasten for his holy blessing, he, with his hands raised, will bless you together with the apostles. If like them you follow, in desire and with tears, the ascending Lord, if with all the others, you yearn to meet and contemplate him, to the admiration of the attending host you will be admitted to the perfectly harmonious heavenly choirs who follow the Lord Jesus Christ unto the interior veils, unto the very presence of God the Father. 'As wax melts before fire,' as a pile of silver is rendered soft by heat, so will your affections overflow your heart. Yearning and pining for the courts of the Lord, you will ascend to God with your whole heart; your whole being will be drawn to him; you will be united to him with all your strength. You will become one with him for all eternity. (pp. 99–100)

Stephen of Sawley sought a mystical death while meditating on the crucifixion and a mystical union while meditating on the ascension. His presentation represents the developed Cistercian tradition, a century after Bernard and his contemporaries, at the point in time when Francis of Assisi took meditation on the passion out of the cloister and into the world at large.

Francis of Assisi (1181/82–1228), founder of the Franciscan order, was praying on Mount La Verna in 1224 when he envisioned a crucified Seraph and received the stigmata that he bore until his death. According to Bonaventure, whose biography of Francis was authorized by a General Chapter of the Franciscan Order in 1260 (Fleming, 1977, pp. 32–72), Francis had been meditating on the passion when he beheld "the vision of a winged Seraph in the form of the Crucified" (Bonaventure, 1978, p. 54):

> Whoever turns his face fully to the Mercy Seat and with faith, hope and love, devotion, admiration, exultation, appreciation, praise and joy beholds him hanging upon the cross, such a one makes the Pasch, that is, the passover, with Christ. By the staff of the cross he passes over the Red Sea, going from Egypt into the desert, where he will taste the *hidden manna*; and with Christ he rests in the tomb, as if dead to the outer world, but experiencing, as far as is possible in this wayfarer's state, what was said on the cross to the thief who adhered to Christ; *Today you shall be with me in paradise.*
>
> This was shown also to blessed Francis, when in ecstatic contemplation on the height of the mountain—where I thought out these things I have written—there appeared to him a six-winged Seraph

fastened to a cross, as I and several others heard in that very place
from his companion who was with him then. There he passed over
into God in ecstatic contemplation and became an example of perfect
contemplation as he had previously been of action. (pp. 111–12)

Bonaventure described Francis's experience as a mystical death that was
followed by an ecstasy of wisdom.

The soul can pass over to peace through ecstatic elevations of
Christian wisdom. There is no other path but through the burning
love of the Crucified, a love which so transformed Paul into Christ
when he *was carried up to the third heaven* (2 Cor. 12:2) that he
could say: *With Christ I am nailed to the cross. I live, now not I, but
Christ lives in me* (Gal. 2:20). This love also so absorbed the soul of
Francis that his spirit shone through his flesh when for two years
before his death he carried in his body the sacred stigmata of the
passion. (pp. 54–55)

Bonaventure described the content of the Seraphic vision more fully as
follows:

On a certain morning about the feast of the Exaltation of the Cross,
while Francis was praying on the mountainside, he saw a Seraph with
six fiery and shining wings descend from the height of heaven. And
when in swift flight the Seraph had reached a spot in the air near the
man of God, there appeared between the wings the figure of a man
crucified, with his hands and feet extended in the form of a cross and
fastened to a cross. Two of the wings were lifted above his head, two
were extended for flight and two covered his whole body. When Francis saw this, he was overwhelmed and his heart was flooded with a
mixture of joy and sorrow. He rejoiced because of the gracious way
Christ looked upon him under the appearance of the Seraph, but the
fact that he was fastened to a cross *pierced his soul with a sword* of com-
passionate sorrow (Luke 2:35).
    He wondered exceedingly at the sight of so unfathomable a vision,
realizing that the weakness of Christ's passion was in no way compat-
ible with the immortality of the Seraph's spiritual nature. Eventually
he understood by a revelation from the Lord that divine providence
had shown him this vision so that, as Christ's lover, he might learn in
advance that he was to be totally transformed into the likeness of
Christ crucified, not by the martyrdom of his flesh, but by the fire of
his love consuming his soul.

As the vision disappeared, it left in his heart a marvelous ardor and imprinted on his body markings that were no less marvelous. Immediately the marks of nails began to appear in his hands and feet just as he had seen a little before in the figure of the man crucified. . . . Also his right side, as if pierced with a lance, was marked with a red wound from which his sacred blood often flowed, moistening his tunic and underwear. (pp. 305–6)

Bonaventure offered little discussion of Francis's practice of meditation on the passion. What was important theologically was the vision of the Seraph. For present purposes, however, I emphasize that as the flying Seraph approached, the figure of a crucified man became visible between its wings. When Francis puzzled out the meaning of the vision, he realized that it pertained to himself. The wounds of the Seraph constituted a prophecy of his own stigmata.

If we understand Bonaventure's description of Francis "as Christ's lover" as a reference to the contemplative experience that medieval writers called the spiritual marriage, we must understand "the figure of a man crucified" as no other than Francis himself. Such an interpretation would be consonant with Bonaventure's understanding of Francis as "the Angel of true peace" who "was . . . assigned an angelic ministry and was totally aflame with a Seraphic fire" (p. 180). Bonaventure explicitly wrote:

And so not without reason is he considered to be symbolized by the image of the Angel who ascends from the sunrise bearing the seal of the living God, in the true prophecy of that other *friend of the Bridegroom,* John the Apostle and Evangelist. For *"when the sixth seal was opened,"* John says in the Apocalypse, *"I saw another Angel ascending from the rising of the sun, having the seal of the living God."* (p. 181)

Through Francis' ministry and Bonaventure's writings, meditation on the passion was popularized throughout Western Christendom. Bonaventure (1217–1274) became the Third Minister General of the Franciscan Order. After Bernard, Bonaventure was the greatest and most influential authority on mysticism in the Latin Church in the High Middle Ages. Through Bonaventure or, more precisely, through Bonaventure's formulation of Francis's approach to Christian mysticism, mystical death and resurrection ceased to be a minor interest of occasional Cistercian monks and instead reached a broader audience.

Bonaventure presented mystical death and resurrection as a total program of Christian mysticism. Other experiences might be admirable but were not necessary. Bonaventure announced his program at the very beginning of *Lignum vitae* (Tree of Life).

With Christ I am nailed to the cross, from Galatians, chapter two. The true worshiper of God and disciple of Christ, who desires to conform perfectly to the Savior of all men crucified for him, should, above all, strive with an earnest endeavor of soul to carry about continuously, both in his soul and in his flesh, the cross of Christ until he can truly feel in himself what the Apostle said above. Moreover an affection and feeling of this kind is merited to be experienced in a vital way only by one who, not unmindful of the Lord's passion nor ungrateful, contemplates the labor, suffering and love of Jesus crucified, with such vividness of memory, such sharpness of intellect and such charity of will that he can truly say with the bride: *A bundle of myrrh is my beloved to me; he will linger between my breasts.* (Bonaventure, 1978, p. 119)

Bonaventure began by quoting Paul, "With Christ I am nailed to the cross." A person was "to conform perfectly" by being "crucified" and "carry[ing] about continuously . . . the cross of Christ." When the individual "can truly feel in himself what the Apostle said above," he no longer meditates, he "contemplates the labor, suffering and love of Jesus crucified." Bonaventure alluded to the experience of Christ's love by quoting from the Song of Songs, which Bernard had interpreted as an allegory of spiritual marriage.

Bonaventure devoted a second text, *Vitis Mystica, seu Tractatus de Passione Domini* (The Mystical Vine, Treatise on the Passion of the Lord) to the specific topic of meditation on the passion. In it, he cited Paul and Bernard as authorities requiring meditators themselves to die with Jesus. Meditation on the passion was not to be conducted from the imagined perspective of an eyewitness of Jesus. The passion was instead to be imagined from Jesus' point of view:

Following the advice of the blessed apostle Paul, let us therefore go forth to our Spouse, Jesus, bountiful and sovereign Goodness, outside of the camp, that is, outside of the concupiscence of this world; bearing with Him the reproach of the cross and the harshness of the bonds. For in the words of Bernard, "it is not fitting that, under a crucified Head, there should be a delicate member"; nor does a member seem to belong to the same body as the head if it has not suffered with the head.

Let us be bound with the bonds of the passion of the good and most loving Jesus, so that we may also share with Him the bonds of love. For, made fast by these latter, he was drawn down from heaven to earth in order to suffer the former. Conversely, we who desire to be drawn from earth into heaven, must bind ourselves to our Head with the bonds of the passion, through which we will attain the bonds of love and thus become one with Him. (Bonaventure, 1960, pp. 161–62).

The meditation that Bonaventure composed for his reader to employ when meditating on the passion runs several pages in print. It is almost entirely written from an indeterminate perspective. However, the final sentences of the passage abruptly contrasted two approaches to meditation on the passion: one that was limited to external appearances, and another that involved conformance with his crucifixion:

> Those who are led only by appearances saw on the cross Him who is *fairer in beauty than the sons of men* deprived of beauty or human sightliness. They saw a disfigured face and a distorted body. Yet from this disfigurement of our Saviour flowed the price of our grace. We have seen, at least in part, the dark and outward ugliness of the body of our most loving Jesus. But who shall tell of the inner beauty of Him in whom *dwells all the fullness of the Godhead?* Let us, too, be deformed outwardly in our bodies, together with Jesus deformed, that we may be reformed internally, to companion Jesus most fair. Let us, in our body, conform to the body of our Vine, so that *the body of our lowliness* may be reformed through conformity *to the body of His glory.* (pp. 164–68)

In this passage, Bonaventure rejected meditation on the passion from the perspective of an eyewitness, and insisted on being crucified with Christ.

Itinerarium Mentis ad Deum (The Mind's Journey into God) is often regarded as Bonaventure's mystical masterpiece. It deals almost entirely with contemplative experiences. However, immediately prior to the prayers that end the text, Bonaventure discussed meditation on the passion as the very last topic of the treatise—as though meditation on the passion were a mystic's final preparation for the passage into God:

> If you wish to know how these things come about, ask grace not instruction, desire not understanding, the groaning of prayer not diligent reading, the Spouse not the teacher, God not man, darkness not clarity, not light but the fire that totally inflames and carries us into God by ecstatic unctions and burning affections. This fire is God, and *his furnace is in Jerusalem*; and Christ enkindles it in the heat of his burning passion which only he truly perceives who says: *My soul chooses hanging and my bones death.* Whoever loves this death can see God because it is true beyond doubt that *man will not see me and live.* Let us, then, die and enter into the darkness; let us impose silence

upon our cares, our desires and our imaginings. With Christ crucified
let us pass *out of this world to the Father.* (Bonaventure, 1978, pp.
115–16).

Only a person who "with Christ crucified" "says: My soul chooses hanging and
my bones death" can see God in a contemplative manner and then progress
beyond contemplation into the darkness of the Father. Bonaventure's reference
to mystical death was unequivocal.

With the passage of the centuries, Bonaventure's meaning came to be lost.
Ewert Cousins (1987, p. 389) accurately paraphrased Bonaventure's theology:
"For him [Bonaventure], Christ's death symbolizes what in recent spiritual
writings has been called the death of the ego, that is, the finite or superficial
self, and the awakening of the deeper self which is united to God." However,
Cousins did not understand Bonaventure's theology in its historical context.
He did not appreciate that in quoting Paul's words, "With Christ I am nailed
to the cross," Bonaventure (1978, p. 97) referred to a vivid, pictorial, and emotional experience of imagining one's own bodily death, that was followed by a
sense of the invisible presence of God *per viam negationis.* By ego death,
Cousins and other contemporary writers refer to an imageless experience in
which there is no sense of personal identity. It is the experience that remains
possible in a state of extremely deep trance when the ego functions of reality-
testing, sense perception, memory, reason, fantasy, and self-representation are
repressed. Scholars who interpret Bonaventure's language to refer to a suspension of the functions of consciousness are mistaken. During mystical death, the
ego functions normally, but consciousness is filled with vivid, emotionally grip-
ping fantasies that portray the self-representation as dying.

What Cousins and others term "ego death" is a very different type of mystical experience. Muslim Sufis call it *fana* (annihilation), and medieval Jewish
kabbalists termed it the "kiss of death" (Fishbane, 1994). The Sufi term was
promoted by Marguerite Porete, whose *Mirror of Simple Souls* speaks of the
soul's "annihilation" through "three entire deaths . . . the death of sin . . . the
death of nature . . . [and] the death of the spirit" (Porete, 1993, pp. 135–36).
The kabbalistic trope entered the Christian world during the Renaissance. For
example, Giordano Bruno (1964, p. 127) discussed "the death of the soul,
called by the Cabalists death of the kiss, symbolized in the Canticle of
Solomon . . . by others this death is called sleep. . . . He then speaks for the
soul as languid inasmuch as it is dead in itself, and alive in its object." The
motif was subsequently adapted by Christian mystics as the soul's death during mystical union and its resurrection upon God's withdrawal (Arbman 1968,
pp. 133–44, 371–73). The metaphor refers to the loss of self-representation
and its replacement by a sense of divine presence at the climax of some mystical experiences. St. Teresa of Avila (1946, I, p. 158) explained that "the soul is

wholly in the power of another, and during that period, which is very short, I do not think that the Lord leaves it freedom for anything."

CONCLUDING REFLECTIONS

Both Bonaventure and Henry Suso referred explicitly to two ways of meditating on the passion. The distinction was part of their self-understanding. The practice that can be traced from Anselm of Canterbury through the third week of Loyola's *Spiritual Exercises* advocated meditation from the imagined perspective of an eyewitness. It overlapped with *lectio divina* and was at best psychohygienic. Building on Widengren's observations, I have traced a second approach to meditation on the passion from Bernard of Clairvaux through Walter Hilton. The second technique meditated on the passion from the imagined perspective of Jesus.

From Bernard onward, meditations on the passion from the imagined perspective of Jesus were understood in terms of Paul's discussions of being crucified with Christ. In the thirteenth century, as the concept of oneness gained currency as a synonym for spiritual marriage, meditation on the passion from the perspective of Jesus was described as an instance of becoming one with Christ. James of Milan wrote that a "man . . . may perfectly be oned to God and changed into him" (Hilton, 1952, p. 146), and similar language was employed in an anonymous addition to the Latin manuscript of *Stimulus amoris* (Hilton, 1952, p. 74). Although the term "mystical death" belongs to the comparative study of religion, it accurately captures the Christian understanding of the phenomenon in the late Middle Ages.

Chapter 5

The Therapeutic Action of Crucifixion with Christ

Unlike secular psychotherapists, Hilton entertained neither a mechanical model of psychic determinism nor an existential approach to voluntary human agency. He instead attributed the soul's reforming in feeling to Jesus. "He does all. He forms and reforms: he forms by himself alone, but he reforms us with us; for all this is done by the giving of grace, and by applying our will to grace" (Hilton, 1991, p. 247). Without affirming or denying that a role is played by grace, we may inquire about the psychological aspects of crucifixion with Christ.

Crucifixion with Christ was a medieval form of guided imagery therapy. The first of the modern guided imagery therapies was the *reve éveillé dirigé* (directed daydream), that Robert Desoille (1966) introduced in 1938. Eugène Caslant (1927) had used the couch and free association to pursue paranormal and clairvoyant investigations that involved images of ascension to other-worldly regions, and Desoille appropriated Caslant's techniques for psychotherapeutic purposes. Desoille's work inspired the philosopher Gaston Bachelard (1987), who used the term "reverie" in reference to guided imagery states in a series of publications that began in 1943 (van der Berg, 1962, pp. 5–6, 9). Bachelard's use of the term "reverie" reached a broad public audience, where it mingled with ideas of daydreaming, creative inspiration, and kindred waking states. The term "reverie" also gained technical use in psychoanalysis through Wilfred R. Bion, but reverie states had been integral to psychoanalytic technique since its innovation. In his first discussion of the practice of free association, Freud (1900) wrote:

> As we fall asleep, 'involuntary ideas' emerge . . . [and] change into visual and acoustic images. . . . In the state used for the analysis of

dreams and pathological ideas, the patient purposely and deliberately abandons this activity and . . . the involuntary thoughts which now emerge . . . —and here the situation differs from falling asleep— retain the character of ideas. *In this way the 'involuntary' ideas are transformed into 'voluntary' ones.* (p. 102; Freud's italics)

With these words Freud explained that free association is performed during a state that resembles the hypnagogic state between waking and sleeping. The patient is asked to report, verbally, whatever may be the contents of consciousness. The act of speaking aloud tends to suppress spontaneously arising imagery through their preconscious translation into spontaneously arising verbal equivalents. Freud's discussion implied that imagery persisted preconsciously and provided a foundation for the therapeutic effects of free association.

Simple attempts at visualization can induce the reverie state that Freud described. Hanscarl Leuner (1984, p. 2), who began to work with guided imagery in 1945, claimed that his technique of Guided Affective Imagery (GAI) was psychoanalytically oriented. To describe the mental images, Leuner used the term "catathymic imagery" that Ernst Meier, a coworker of Eugen Bleuler, had coined. Meier derived the term from Greek *kata* (dependent) and *thymos* (soul or emotionality) (Leuner, 1978, p. 125). Leuner (1984) found that an extremely large percentage of persons can achieve catathymic images (p. 6). "The mere instruction to imagine can gradually diminish the waking consciousness, which again deepens the imagination in a circular process" (p. 16). The onset of the alternate state is signaled by the shift from daydream imagery to catathymic imagery:

Their special quality lies in their colorfulness, plasticity, and emotional impact in contrast to the simple imaginings, which we have in everyday experience, when we recall a scene from the past in our imagination. As everyone can easily verify, these simple imaginal products are generally pale, colorless, and considerably easier to influence. It is an unusual feature of catathymic images that in full form they no longer obey the will. On the contrary, they follow an autonomous course. This course can be explained by unconscious impulses . . . that direct the imaginings. (pp. 13–14)

Catathymic images resemble hypnagogic hallucinations that occur immediately prior to falling asleep (p. 15), but they differ in that a waking reverie state is maintained voluntary (as is also the case in free association). The images are pseudo-hallucinations, that is, hallucinations that are known to be such. Leuner (1969) explained:

The patient's state of consciousness is similar to that which occurs in meditative states. It is often surprising to hear him excitedly describe vivid colors and detailed forms which are experienced as parts of a totally new world. The patient paradoxically seems to be living in this fantasy world while he simultaneously knows that he is doing this with his therapist for purposes of treatment. It is this experience of a "quasi-reality" with its concomitant feelings and associated affects, occurring within a state of altered consciousness, that we call catathymic imagery. This enhancement of emotions is the most important component of the therapeutic process. (pp. 5–6)

Catathymic imagery has been studied and used in psychotherapies from many points of view. Kubie (1943) used hypnagogic reveries to access repressed memories as an adjunct to psychoanalysis. Other psychoanalytic approaches include inducing the reverie state and then working analytically with whatever images are produced spontaneously (Reyher, 1977, 1978). In other cases, images from a previous night's dream have been treated as a point of departure. Silverman (1987) invited analysands to image, rather than to associate verbally, during the working through phase of psychoanalysis; he then interpreted the emotionally rich imagery. Leuner's "Guided Affective Imagery" (GAI), which used a standard series of ten images (Krojanker, 1966; Leuner, 1969, 1975, 1977, 1978, 1984), most closely approximates the medieval program of envisioning a standard narrative sequence.

At the same time, Leuner's work remained within the psychoanalytic tradition. He had imagers begin each session with a predetermined motif, but he was interested primarily in individual variations and spontaneous developments of the images. Leuner (1984) recognized that catathymic imagery may be beneficial, but may instead have a negative character (pp. 34, 54, 95). Whenever possible he allowed imagers to resolve emotionally difficult developments on their own. He intervened only when imagers needed his assistance. He developed a series of interventions in order to direct the images toward therapeutic outcomes, apparently on a trial-and-error basis that is consistent with the psychoanalytic procedure that Robert Langs (1978, 1994) has more recently termed "unconscious supervision."

When a suggestion or an interpretation by the therapist is relevant to the meaning of the patient's imagery, it is followed by a sudden transformation of the picture. This apparently occurs because of the sensitivity of GAI imagery to every small change in emotions, whether conscious or not. . . . These "microdiagnostic" manifestations reflect the course of even the smallest details of the therapeutic process. In this way, GAI can be used as a check on the likely influence of any therapeutic gambit or spontaneous influence on the patient's psyche before he shows any behavioral change. (Leuner, 1969, pp. 13–14)

The effectiveness of guided imagery therapies depends on the same principles that underlie successful religious healing. Oskar Pfister long ago recognized that religious healing can successfully promote psychotherapeutic change, as gauged by psychoanalytic standards, when the religious practices happen to deploy religious symbolism in fashions that the unconscious superego can use to achieve insights:

> How can the unconscious, making use of symbols, lay bare the symptoms? Let us remember that every symptom arises from a repressed inner conflict and that it makes use of disguises to spare the unconscious annoyance. In these religious ceremonies the unconscious of the medicine man speaks to the unconscious of his patient and circumvents consciousness. He thus avoids resistance which would have been aroused, had consciousness intervened.
>
> The dissolution of that conflict which had been solved in an unsatisfactory manner by the disease symptom is accomplished by this influence of one unconscious on another. . . . The repressed Superego assumes the responsibility of dissolving this conflict, and the motive for retaining the symptom ceases to exist. (Pfister, 1932, p. 251)

By the repressed superego, Pfister referred to the unhealthy repression of unconscious conscience. He was not discussing the so-called savage superego, which is a preconscious process that is never subject to repression.

The therapeutic action of religious healing (see also: Devereux, 1958; Merkur, 1995–96, 2004, 2005; Haartman, 2004) is precisely parallel to the use of symbolism in play therapy. Both procedures rest on an unconscious process that Freud (1913) had noted:

> Psychoanalysis has shown us that everyone possesses in his unconscious mental activity an apparatus which enables him to interpret other people's reactions, that is, to undo the distortions which other people have imposed on the expression of their feelings. (p. 259)

Leuner's (1984, p. 95) interventions frequently proceeded from the post-Kleinian assumption that all of the characters in catathymic imagery are manifestations of introjects that are split-off parts of the self. Leuner recommended that therapeutic interventions aim at the integration of the introjects within the self. Desoille's (1966) interventions, by contrast, had proceeded from an implicitly behavioristic assumption. When a menacing figure confronted an imager, Desoille discouraged flight and urged that the figure be attacked and defeated. It may be appreciated that different client populations benefit, and fail to derive benefit, from differing strategies of intervention.

Medieval crucifixions with Christ differed from modern guided imagery therapies by involving a complete narrative that was composed of a sequence of narrative episodes that followed a set dramatic course. Crucifixions with Christ were not meditated as a sequence of single images that were allowed to unfold as they would. There was comparatively little opportunity for the spontaneous occurrence of original narrative materials. This difference between the two procedures imposed corresponding constraints on the interpretations that guided the imagery to become therapeutic. Modern practices depend on therapists who make interpretations in response to patients' spontaneous deviations from the set images. For example, a guided imagery therapist might suggest envisioning a meadow. The patient would then supply images such as sunshine and a light breeze, or a thunderstorm and bitter cold, or something else; and the therapist would analyze the imagery that the patient added to the guided images. Medieval meditations involved neither spontaneous deviations nor their interpretations. All of the images were predetermined by the meditations. For therapeutic interpretations to be attached to the images, they had to be integral to the drama of the Christ story. The interpretations were contained within the narrative, as parts of the story itself. Because meditations on the passion were not transformative unless they contained the specific element of crucifixion with Christ, we must additionally postulate that the interpretations within the passion narrative did not lead to mutative insights unless they were experienced from Jesus' point of view.

How did the meditations accomplish their ends?

SELF-FOCUS AND SPLITTING

The therapeutic principles underlying crucifixion with Christ have perhaps their closest psychoanalytic parallel in the concepts of Klein (1935, 1937, 1940) and Winnicott (1948, 1950–55, 1952, 1954–55) who discussed the therapeutic acquisition of a capacity to bear guilt, feel concern, and make reparation. There is no immediate reason to enter into the unearned assumption, shared by Klein and Winnicott, that the sequence that we observe in the clinical progress of adult patients is necessarily the same sequence that occurs in health during childhood. Klein (1935, p. 276n) introduced her concept of a "position," in preference to terms such as "mechanism" or "phase," in order to account for "the quick change-over that occurs from a persecution anxiety or depressed feeling to a normal attitude" in both children and adults; and it suffices to trace the core of Klein's egregiously named "paranoid-schizoid" and "depressive positions" by reference to Martin Buber's philosophy of *I and Thou* ([1917] 1958). Buber suggested that we all approach other people sometimes as an "It" and sometimes as a "Thou," and that we go back and forth between "I-It" and "I-Thou" relations all day, everyday. From a psychoanalytic perspective, the question of health and pathology depends on a person's ability to navigate back and forth between the two modes of relating whenever it is reasonable to do so. The one mode of relating is appropriate in some situations, and the other in others.

For present purposes, it is simplest to speak of the one mode as self-focussed and the other as concerned with interpersonal relations. Consider, for example, Money-Kyrle's (1944) description of the varieties of moral motivation.

> [There are] three fundamental subjective principles of primary morality: It is bad (i.e., it arouses guilt) to injure or threaten a good object; it is good to love, repair and defend a good object; it is also good to hate, attack or destroy a bad object, that is, any thing or person that threatens to destroy a good one. (pp. 186–87)

Only the second orientation, which loves, repairs and defends good objects, is concerned to maintain an interpersonal relationship. The first, that it is bad to harm a good object, makes no connection with the object; while the third, that it is good to aggress against a bad object, aims at destroying the very prospect of relationship. Whether, in any given circumstance, their objectives are justified, their concern is with burning bridges, not with building them. They make instrumental use of people, they do not engage them interpersonally.

Self-focus, a term that I prefer to Symington's (1993, p. 118; 1994, p. 126) extension of the concept of "narcissism," is a conscious phenomenon that is highly variable in content: the tunnel vision of depressives' emptiness and self-recriminations, hysterics' sense of victimization and self-pity, obsessive-compulsives' preoccupation with their drivenness, the different grandiosities of narcissists and paranoiacs, and so forth. Whatever its content, self-focus is largely unaware of other people. Self-focus can be oblivious and unconcerned rather than avoidant or hostile. It limits the conscious perception of others to their utility as extensions of self. They become "subjectively perceived objects" (Winnicott, 1960, 1963b) or "selfobjects" that are idealized when they are compliant but are angrily hated and derogated when they are recognized as acting independently (Kohut, 1966, 1971, 1977). Through self-focus, other people are reduced, in Buber's term, to an "It."

Integral to self-focus is a failure to evaluate other people in their own right. Objects are instead rated as good or bad from the exclusive perspective of the self. The result is an unconscious splitting of realistic perceptions through the generation of a pair of opposing fantasies: idealization, on the one hand, and an equally excessive devaluation on the other. Identification with the idealization lends a grandiosity to the conscious self-focus; the grandiosity is termed "inflation" by C. G. Jung (1952, p. 315; see also Whitmont 1969, p. 59), "the manic defense" by Kleinians, and "narcissism" by Symington (1993). The devaluation tends at the same time to be projected onto other people, who become objects of derogation, hate, contempt, fear, condescension, and so forth.

A further component of the "narcissistic constellation," as Symington (1993) termed it, is unconscious guilt:

> The essence of narcissism lies in an emotional refusal. . . . The consequence of this refusal is guilt, which is not available to consciousness. . . . This manifests itself in a variety of ways: people bring down on their head disasters of one sort or another. . . .
>
> Inwardly, people judge themselves to be bad—so bad that they cannot bear to experience it, so they have to seduce the world into telling them they are good. (Symington, 1994, p. 123)

Symington (1993, p. 39; 2001, p. 42) maintained that the emotional refusal that is involved in narcissism is a refusal both of other people and of the person of the Absolute. Unconscious knowledge of the refusal produces guilt that is valid, but the refusal causes the valid guilt to be replaced in consciousness by a pathological guilt that is irrational but symptomatic of the syndrome.

> Where there is neurotic guilt or psychotic guilt, there is also real guilt that cannot be borne. Also, in such a case, conscience is stifled and replaced by a savage superego. (Symington, 2004, p. 78)

> The savage super-ego is reproaching the ego for something. What emerges from psychoanalytic investigation is that the savage attacks of the super-ego are always present where the other as a feeling person is obliterated. (Symington, 1994, p. 156)

To Symington's formulation, I add that the primary refusal pertains to the mother. The repression of the mother's personhood—in Fonagy's terminology, the inhibition of mentalization, or attributing mind to the mother (Fonagy et al., 2002)—commits the manifest personality to a narcissism, lacking in empathy, that shapes all other object relations, whether real or imaginary. The impact of narcissism on theism may include atheism, but it may instead lead to the conception of an impersonal divine substance or being, or to instrumental or exploitative uses of supernatural beings.

Meditation on the passion encouraged intense emotional involvement with splitting. In the passion story, splitting is represented most prominently by Jesus and his murderers. Jesus is idealized as the sinless lamb; the Jews and the Gentile executioners are demonized as the worst of all possible people. Consider the following passage from Bonaventure's *The Mystical Vine*:

After casting You out of the vineyard, that is, the city or society of men, these sacrilegious vine tenders killed You. And not with one blow: they put You to the slow torture of the cross and of the countless wounds made by the scourges and the nails.

O tender Jesus, how many are those who strike You? You are struck by Your Father, *who has not spared even His own Son*, but has delivered You for us all; You strike Yourself, for You have delivered up to death Your life, which none can take from You but Yourself; Your disciple strikes You by his treason and his deceitful kiss; the Jews strike You with blows on the body and face, and the Gentiles with scourges and nails! Behold how many times You have been struck and humiliated; how many were those who struck You!

And how many, also, are those who deliver You up! You are offered up by Your own Father, who has delivered You for us all; You offer Yourself up, as one of Your servants says in an outburst of gratitude: He *loved us and delivered Himself up for us*. O wonderful commerce! The Lord gives Himself up for the servant, God for man, the Creator for His creature, the Innocent for the sinner! For You have surrendered Yourself into the hands of the betrayer, the false disciple, Judas; the betrayer sold you to the Jews; the Jews, in turn, wretched betrayers also, delivered You up to the Gentiles to be mocked and spit upon, to be scourged and crucified. You told and foretold these things, and they came to pass. When all had been fulfilled, behold, You were crucified and *reckoned among the wicked*. Wound You was not enough for them: they had *to add to the pain of Him* they had wounded, by giving You wine mixed with myrrh and gall to drink in Your thirst. (Bonaventure, 1960, pp. 165–66)

Here we can see that splitting was integral to the passion narrative. The doctrine that Christ and God the Father are two persons of the one Trinity was unmentioned. Jesus was instead counterposed with the Father, who delivered him up. Rage and hate toward God, was, however, an impiety that could not be countenanced consciously. The rage and hatred were made devotionally acceptable through their redirection toward the Jews and the Roman soldiers whose villainy was integral to the passion narrative. Splitting may again be seen in the oversight of the historical reality that Jesus of Nazareth was a Jew, which makes Christian anti-Semitism self-contradictory.

Anti-Semitism has traditionally been integral to the interior emotional logic of the Christian myth (Ostow, 1996), because it brings to consciousness the ugly, sinful, unchristian sentiments that Christians routinely harbor, attempt to control, and suffer guilt over. In providing an outlet for aggression, anti-Semitism provides an emotional corrective for Christian afterlife beliefs. Discussing the fear of death, Zilboorg (1943) suggested:

> Religious feelings are utilized for . . . self-inflationary denial of death. . . . The affect of fear is repressed and lost in self-inflationary cheer. . . . The passive communion with God and the eternal, immortal forces of the world . . . reinforce the unconscious fantasy of corporeal immortality and thus reduce the death anxiety. (pp. 471–73)

To maintain belief in the postmortem prospect of heaven, where there is no sorrow, but also no rage and no hatred, Christians must keep themselves from feeling loss, sorrow, fear, and anger over the prospect of death. The inappropriate and false cheer that surrounds afterlife beliefs, for example, at funerals, is an instance, in psychoanalytic terms, of the manic defense (Winnicott, 1935), a happiness that masks an underlying depressiveness. Because the depression is intolerable, bringing the unconscious fear of death into consciousness, as is necessary if the fear is to be resolved, requires a mobilization of aggression (Zilboorg, 1943, p. 473). Meditations on the passion used anti-Semitism and outrage against Roman soldiers to trigger rage and hatred that ended the false cheer of the manic defense. The aggression was consciously directed against the murderers who were blamed for the necessity of Jesus' death; but unconsciously the rage was also directed against Jesus, whose self-sacrifice brought the issue to crisis. The anger at Jesus was kept unconscious, at least in part, by the doctrine of original sin, which directed rage and hatred against the self. By requiring conscious meditations on hatred and self-hatred, meditation on the passion helped arouse the fear of death that would ordinarily be denied and kept unconscious by recourse to Christian afterlife beliefs.

Meditation on the passion from the imagined perspective of an eyewitness would have have brought the fear of death to consciousness, but it may also be assumed to have intensified splitting. Christian doctrine holds that Jesus was crucified in order to redeem humanity from the consequences of original sin. In this respect, Jesus is idealized as the good Son, never rebellious, who obeys his Father even to death. But the same narrative has unstated, split-off, unconscious implications. Why must Jesus die in order that humanity be saved? And who has the power to impose so evil a necessity on God the Son? Jesus' willingness to endure a crucifixion that he prophesied was not only an active embrace of martyrdom. It is also understood unconsciously as a wish for suicide. Most suicide attempts are unsuccessful because their purpose is not to end life but to shame the living; and this common human motive for suicide is reasonably treated as a common unconscious understanding of the passion. Unconsciously, Christians recognize the passion as a suicide, and they understand it in the common manner. Jesus achieves victory through his suicide. The intended target of shame is God the Father, a merciless, autocratic tyrant who refused to forgive original sin until Jesus shamed him. No one but Jesus would dare to oppose the Father, and nothing less than Jesus' death could shame the Father into having compassion. Importantly, the unconscious understanding that Jesus used suicide to shame is a projection of self-focus. In submitting to crucifixion, Jesus is unconsciously imagined to treat God the Father is an "It" to be shamed, and not as a "Thou" who is to be encountered in an interpersonal relationship.

As we have seen, individuals such as the author of *Ancrene Wisse*, Marguerete Porete, St. Edmund of Canterbury, and the Monk of Farne varied in the severity of their reaction to the mix of guilt and gratitude that their meditations induced, but meditations regularly intensified the blend. For some, the meditations served to exacerbate their neuroses, pushing the practitioners to ever more intense feats of asceticism. In their cases, the personal, psychological conflicts that found culturally congenial symbolism in the impersonal imagery of the passion found no resolution. We may assume their meditations were more akin to pathological repetition compulsions than to the mild catharsis of healthy play. There was no abreaction, no mourning, no embrace of humanity in compassion and altruism, no joy in the world of God's creation. Instead, there was unrelieved grieving and unceasing efforts to atone through self-denial. Doctrinal reasons, which is to say, socially acceptable, stereotypical rationalizations for the guilt included guilt over original sin; guilt in needing ransom by Christ, at such cruel cost to Jesus; and guilt over sinful thoughts and fantasies. Personal guilt of a neurotic nature may nevertheless be presumed to have been at work.

RELATIONAL THINKING

The mode of thinking that Klein termed the "depressive position" and Winnicott called the "phase of concern," I attribute to relational thinking (Merkur, 2001b). Relational thinking is a conscious and unconscious superego function that involves a capacity to know that another person is another person, who exists in his or her own right, has his or her own feelings, motives, goals, history, and hopes, and in general is a complete human being, comparable to oneself. Relational thinking includes imitation, mentalization, role-taking, empathy, concern, conscience, altruism, and so forth.

Where the self-focus of neurotic thinking constructs God as a "subjectively perceived object" (Winnicott, 1960, 1963b), relational thinking engages God as a whole object or objectively perceived object. In Buber's terms, this represents a shift from regarding God as an It to encountering God as a Thou. Precisely such a transition from self-focused splitting to relational thinking is what little we can discern with confidence of the therapeutic action of the conversion of St. Paul. Although the conversion of Paul has been paradigmatic for Christianity, the discrepancies among its three versions indicate a blend of history and legend that makes its details uncertain (Stanley, 1953; Bornkamm, 1971, pp. 13–25; Lohfink, 1976; Hedrick, 1981). Paul's account of his ascension to heaven (II Cor 12:1–9) reveals that he was deeply versed in Jewish visionary practices of his era (Segal, 1980, 1990; Tabor, 1986; Morray-Jones, 1993a, 1993b). The allusions to Ezekiel in Paul's account of his conversion before Agrippa, Bernice, and Festus (Acts 26:17–18; see Stanley, 1953, p. 333) similarly places Paul among the Jewish *merkabah* mystics who attempted to envision the divine chariot-throne described in Ezekiel 1. The *Acts of the Apostles* was almost certainly wrong in attributing Paul's conversion to a vision that occurred spontaneously. His conversion vision should instead be regarded as the high point of a practice of mysticism that had begun considerably earlier. Saul's vision on the road to Damascus was presumably cultivated with the expectation of a vision that would have orthodox Pharisaic content. On this occasion, however, the contents of Saul's vision were unexpected. Here was Saul of Tarsus, busily hunting and delivering people to cruel punishment out of piety to the God of the Pharisees, whose self-focus was abruptly interrupted by a voice that addressed him in the second person.

> Now as he was going along and approaching Damascus, suddenly a light from heaven flashed around him. He fell to the ground and heard a voice saying to him, "Saul, Saul, why do you persecute me?" He asked, "Who are you, Lord?" The reply came, "I am Jesus, whom you are persecuting." (Acts of the Apostles 9:3–5a)

Saul's blinding vision and psychomotor collapse were symptoms of repressed guilt. After the sensory and motor symptoms forced symbolism of guilt into consciousness, the idea of guilt began to manifest directly in the form of a voice that spoke in rebuke. We may attribute both the symbols and the verbalization of guilt to Saul's conscience or, in classical psychoanalytic terms, to his superego. Object relations theory adds further details. From the first word spoken, the voice within his vision engaged Saul in interpersonal relations: "Saul, Saul, why do you persecute me?" The passive capacity to experience an interpersonal relation in a conscious vision enabled Saul to exert the same capacity in an active role. He was able to respond to the voice, addressing it in the second person: "Who are you, Lord?" Because Saul's self-focus had been broken, his splitting collapsed. The voice whom Saul addressed as Lord no longer idealized the God of the Pharisees while demonizing Christians. The idealization and derogation came together in a synthesis that was symbolized by the statement, "I am Jesus, whom you are persecuting." Once Saul achieved a capacity for interpersonal relations within the manifest content of his vision of Jesus, he was able to apply the capacity in his dealings with other people. He abandoned heresy-hunting and instead became a proselytizer.

Whether the legend of Saul on the road to Damascus preserves a record of history or is instead a well-wrought fiction, it is true to life. It was presumably modelled on someone's real experience. For present purposes it is unimportant whether the experience on which the narrative is based occurred to Saul of Tarsus or to someone else, who used his experience as a basis for a tale about the conversion of St. Paul. In either event, the conversion was portrayed as the resolution of an emotionally intolerable conflict. Whether the resolution is attributed to an actual encounter with Jesus, to creative problem-solving, or to divine grace facilitating unconscious creativity, its therapeutic action depended on an assertion of emotional logic. The conversion experience manifested an emotional wholeness and integrity of purpose that Saul, in his conflictedness, had previously lacked.

Writing in 1910 to Pfister, who was both a psychoanalyst and a Lutheran priest, Freud discussed the basic premise of the therapeutic action that I describe: "Things are easier for you than for us physicians, because you can sublimate the transference on to religion and ethics, which is not easy for the invalids of life" (Freud & Pfister, 1963, pp. 39–40). Again, in 1918, Freud wrote: "As for the possibility of sublimation to religion, therapeutically I can only envy you" (p. 63). Because conflicted parental imagos can remain fixated and concrete at the same time that unconflicted aspects of the imagos are depersonified through their sublimation into ego ideals (Jacobson, 1964), therapy can address the sublimated versions of the imagos with much less resistance than the repressed aspects elicit. One may speak, for example, of the wrath of God more easily than of repressed memories of parental rage. The conscious work of analysis is unconsciously understood, however, at the less accessible, latent register of the conflicted parental imagos, permitting therapeutic integration to proceed. In this way, when God functions as a "transferential figure" (Arlow, in Grossman, 1993, p. 760), analysts can use theological analyses of the God representation as vehicles for sublimated interpretations of the transference. This use of religious discourse in psychoanalysis has its analog in self-analysis. When a religious person meditates on religious issues, the sublimated equivalent of a self-analysis may be accomplished, resulting in insight that manifests in a dream or vision, as we have seen in the conversion legend of St. Paul.

Similar principles of therapeutic action can be observed in medieval crucifixions with Christ. In meditations on the passion, both the idealization of
Jesus and the demonization of the Jews and the Roman soldiers may be understood as symptoms that symbolize split-off aspects of the object relation with
God. Bonaventure's *Mystical Vine* mentioned God the Father in passing; but
unconsciously it was the relation with the Father that was at issue throughout.
Klein suggested that the infant's inability to conceptualize mother as an entire
person leads the infant to phantasize a perfect, provident "good breast"
together with its opposite, a totally frustrating "bad breast." Fairbairn (1952)
suggested that the mother both is conceptualized as an entire person and is
split into an exciting object and a rejecting object. In both theories, the
demonic figure cannot be abandoned as long as attachment to the idealized
imago is maintained. As a transferential figure, God becomes heir to the paired
parental projections. In addition, God, who is unconsciously treated, at the
pre-Oedipal level, as both the good mother and the bad mother, is treated at
the Oedipal level as both the good mother and bad father—and their reversals
—the bad mother and good father.

NARRATIVE AND EXPERIENCE

A transition from self-focus to relational thinking is integral to the narrative of
the passion. Luke represented the crucified Christ as saying, "Father, forgive
them, for they do not know what they are doing" (23:34). Pride might be attributed to Jesus upon his royal entrance into Jerusalem, anger when he cleansed the
Temple, and bitterness when he prophesied its destruction. Splitting came to an
end, however, as he faced death on the cross. He felt abandoned by his God, yet
he expressed forgiveness and compassion for his murderers.

Although Jesus manifested a capacity for relational thinking, Christians
ordinarily maintain an emotional distance from the narrative. *Imitateo Christi*
is highly conflicted; it is too much to accomplish. What was good for the God-
man to perform cannot be expected of an ordinary mortal. Moreover, in traditional Christian exegesis, Jesus' compassion for his murderers was consistent
with the compassion for humanity that led him to ransom humanity at the cost
of his own death. Through original sin, all of humanity was implicated in Jesus'
death, bearing responsibility for causing its necessity. Truly to embrace *imitateo Christi* is simultaneously to embrace guilt over the death of Christ. Much
as the one attracts, the other repels.

The result tends most frequently to be a reaction-formation, a configuration of splitting that allocates idealization to consciousness while maintaining
derogation at a preconscious level. The result is hypocrisy. A series of virtues
are espoused consciously, but opposing vices are harbored preconsciously. The

vices are said to be preconscious, rather than unconscious, because they are in open evidence. Christian piety, for example, may be surrounded with jealousy, envy, pride, authoritarianism, judgmentalism, condescension, and a host of obvious but unrepented sins. For example, in the ordinary course of Christian devotion by meditators on the passion, sincere efforts to avoid hypocrisy arrive at severe efforts at self-control. The reaction-formations stay in place, but heroic efforts are made to avoid acting on sinful feelings. So far as possible, the preconscious is suppressed, and the personality impoverished in the process. Asceticism and other self-denials afford measures of temporary relief from the guilt by punishing sinful feelings that remain unavoidable. Reaction-formations, involving unresolved anxiety and guilt, are typical of neurosis (Bergler, 1949, 1959). As well, doctrines that define healthy natural urges as sins, such as traditional Christian attitudes to sexuality in fantasy and behavior, may exacerbate the syndrome of guilt and its management through reaction-formations.

As long as Jesus' capacity for relational thinking provides content for conscious idealization, it is felt to be a thing apart from personality. It may be an obligation, or an unattainable ambition, but it is not part of a Christian's sense of self. It is not who the individual is. It is who Jesus is. It is who saints are, but it is not within reach of the average person. Jesus and saints may love all humanity, but most people do not. Most people can admire love for humanity, and can feel guilt over their failures to achieve love for humanity. However, they cannot make themselves feel as they would wish. A person who meditated from the perspective of an eyewitness would be encouraged by the biblical narrative to feel guilt, sorrow, regret, and gratitude as a recipient of the compassion of Jesus. He might attempt to feel a Christlike compassion for sinners, but he might not. A person who instead meditated from the perspective of Jesus would be guaranteed to make the attempt to feel forgiveness and compassion, but a brief exercise of feeling compassion would not have the power to effect longterm personality change. For Jesus' capacity for interpersonal relations to be integrated as a capacity of one's own, a Christian would have to undergo a therapeutic transformation that corresponded more or less well to the imagined portrait of the passion narrative. The reaction-formation would have to be resolved, and hypocrisy not merely suppressed but uprooted. There would have to be an internal growth, an achievement of increased integrity and authenticity, that permitted the adoption of appropriate cultural models in order to enculturate the achievement.

As a cultural standard, the story of Christ is significant for its portrait of a capacity for relational thinking. In the absence of therapeutic transformations, Christians know its ideas, but many do not feel for the ideas in a deeply personal manner. They may yearn for deep personal feeling, but they do not necessarily achieve the internal growth that generates the feelings. Medieval practices of meditation enhanced the emotional impact of the narrative; but emotional engagement with the narrative was not of itself therapeutic. The emotional engagement was presumably mostly vicarious, as, for example, is the catharsis that is felt by an audience during a theatrical performance. Individuals only rarely respond to the theatre with grief, understanding, mourning, and consolation that is comparable to a healing moment in psychotherapy. People only change when they are ready for therapeutic change. Psychoanalysts go to considerable lengths in order to bring patients to conditions of preparedness for change. The story of the passion contains healthy ideas, but the actualization of their therapeutic effect cannot be explained by the narrative alone.

We have a great many psychoanalytic formulations of the modes of thinking that I have termed self-focus and relational thinking, but very little has been written of the transition between the two. Clinical discussions have addressed interpretations that analysts offer in order to precipitate therapeutic change: talk about the phenomenon of splitting, the unreality of idealization and derogation, the unconscious imagos of the good and bad breast, the penis, vagina, and anus, and so forth. Crucifixion with Christ confronts us with another circumstance. Neither idealization nor derogation was ever challenged, nor was sexual explicitness tolerated.

The transition from self-focus to interpersonal relations was accomplished in a manner that differs from current clinical techniques. The conversion legend of Paul indicates, however, that the spontaneous manifestation of unconscious superego materials during a visionary state may bring the ego into communication with the superego and inaugurate a capacity for interpersonal relations. Was meditation on the passion from the perspective of Christ able to provoke superego manifestations that meditations from the perspectives of eyewitnesses could not?

For therapeutic change to occur, the crucial variable is whether the unconscious relationality of the superego (Merkur, 2001b) is inhibited by the ego's resistance, resulting in the substitute formations of a savage superego, or, the superego succeeds in manifesting consciously, resulting in increased integration of the personality. By the superego, I refer to Freud's (1914a, 1921, 1933) conception of a psychic agency that produces the functions of self-observation, conscience, and ego ideals. The unity of the agency is indicated by the function of conscience, which combines self-observation with ego ideals, or values, in its production of value judgments on the self and others. At the same time, the complication of conscience by neurosis may result in a neurotically severe conscience. Freud's vivid but overly simple phrase "savage superego" notwithstanding, morbid conscience is a compromise of the superego with morbidity, to which the id, ego, and superego all contribute. The superego itself is neither responsible for, nor limited to, morbid conscience. Indeed, the therapeutic process I describe in the conversion of St. Paul and medieval meditation on the passion consists of a transformation of morbid conscience into healthy conscience, through the alleviation of the morbid inhibitions within the preconscious ego that had been forcing morbid distortions on healthy superego manifestations.

Paul's transition, in Winnicott's (1963a) terms, from ruthlessness to a capacity for concern constituted a shift from the fault-finding of a morbid conscience, to a healthy integration of conscience with the ego. The transition was accomplished through a superego manifestation that precipitated guilt long enough for self-observation to recognize that the guilt was survivable (compare: Winnicott, 1969, pp. 105-6). No longer afraid to feel guilt, the ego abandoned further efforts at resistance and integrated conscience within consciousness. The process might reasonably be called a cathartic abreaction of repressed guilt.

The therapeutic transition from a morbid conscience to a healthy integration of the ego and the superego can be precipitated, as St. Paul's conversion exemplifies, through a manifestation of superego symbolism. By resorting to symbol-formation, the superego can always manifest consciously, although in disguised forms that accommodate the ego's resistance. In such cases, the therapeutic shift from a morbid to a healthy conscience sometimes requires nothing more than an interpretation of the manifest content of the superego symbolism that permits conscious integration of the superego's unconscious relationality. In Paul's case, for example, the image of Jesus accusing him of persecution was immediately self-evident as a metaphor that pertained to Paul's persecution not of Christ in heaven, but of Christians on earth. By combining unconscious symbol formation with conscious self-reflection, Paul's superego was able to circumvent his ego's resistance. Encoding communications always makes it possible for the superego to smuggle objectionable materials past the resistance into consciousness, where the communications are sometimes decoded through self-analysis. In other cases, we know that an analyst's verbal interpretations can similarly tip the scale in favor of the conscious manifestation of unconscious materials.

There is no reason to doubt that the scale can be systematically tipped in other manners as well. The medieval evidence suggests that experiences of mystical death were decisive in promoting therapeutic change. How did they precipitate the work of therapy?

Mystical Death as a Crisis of Conscience

Early twelfth century writers developed a theory of mystical death. Bernard of Clairvaux (2000) attributed its fear and terror to the flesh, "since it is natural for the flesh to be terrified by death" (p. 384). If we interpolate the categorical opposition of spirit and the flesh in traditional readings of Paul, Bernard's theory comes to agreement with the formulation of William of St. Thierry, who discussed meditation on the passion in his treatise, *On Contemplating God.* William wrote:

> But when in my eagerness I would approach him . . . I want to see and touch the whole of him and—what is more—to approach the most holy wound in his side, the portal of the ark that is there made, and that not only to put my finger or my whole hand into it, but wholly enter into Jesus' very heart, into the holy of holies, the ark of the covenant, the golden urn, the soul of our humanity that holds within itself the manna of the Godhead—*then,* alas! I am told "Touch me not!" and I hear that word from the Book of Revelation: "Dogs outside!"
>
> Thus, and deservedly, my conscience harries and chastises me, forcing me to pay the penalty for my presumption and my wickedness. Then I return to my rock, the rock that is a refuge for the hedge-hogs that bristle all over with sins. And once again I embrace and kiss your right hand that covers and protects me. (William, 1970, pp. 38–39)

Meditation on the passion of Jesus was implicitly the means "to approach the most holy wound in his side." In seeking to enter the holy of holies, the soul would be refused entry, would be chastised by conscience, and only afterward would return to the rock of its salvation. Through this series of images, William discussed the relation between meditation on the passion and the spiritual marriage. When meditation on the passion led to an adverse experience, it was because "my conscience harries and chastises me, forcing me to pay the penalty for my presumption and my wickedness." In another passage, William addressed Jesus: "the nails of fear of you pierce me" (p. 119). What frightened the flesh, causing it to fear death and divine judgment, was a chastisement of conscience. When conscience had nothing to chastise, meditation led instead to euphoric considerations.

William's theory that mystical death is a chastisement of conscience may be coordinated with a psychoanalytic understanding. I have elsewhere suggested that mystical death closely resembles a panic attack (Merkur, 1992). Although panic attacks include somatic symptoms, fear of imminent death is prominent and frequently takes vivid, pseudohallucinatory form. The analogy with pathological panic attacks should not be pressed unduly. Differing from panic disorder, which involves the repeated occurrences of panic attacks, are the occasional occurrence of a single or a very few panic attacks during psychoanalysis as a manifestation of the transference neurosis (Foxe, 1942; Silber, 1989). Silber (1989) explained that these panic attacks are indices of therapeutic progress:

The abreactive aspect of these "panic attacks" constituted the reliving and thus the remembering in the transference of significant "unconstrained" experiences from the past. . . . the revived affective state of panic, newly constituted as part of the transference neurosis, can act to *facilitate* the patient's recall of an important aspect of her repressed past. In this instance, her panic attacks, or "attacks of terror" as the patient labeled them, represented the *affective content* of several childhood experiences that had been only dimly appreciated during her early years. . . . The return of these disorganized states, manifested as panic attacks, gave her the opportunity to remember, recognize, acknowledge, organize, integrate, understand, and finally master these disruptive episodes. (Silber, 1989, pp. 357, 361)

In his study of early British Methodism, Haartman (2004, pp. 61–70) noted that the prolonged depressions, panic attacks, and dissociative phenomena that attended repentance were precipitated by conflicted attitudes toward God. The desire to surrender to a good and loving God was complicated by guilt, producing unconscious fear and rage at the prospect of God's retaliation. The expectation of retaliation, which was discouraged by Methodist preaching of God's loving welcome of penitents, constituted a negative transference onto God. Both unconscious aggression against one or both parents and unconscious guilt over the aggressive wishes were displaced onto God. In the intense experience of loving and feeling beloved that attends conversion, both the anger and the guilt intensified. The anger sometimes manifested in enactments that were considered backsliding into sinfulness. The guilt, which is self-anger, produced depressions, panic attacks, and dissociations. The intensification of aggression through the transference onto God permitted repressed aggression to manifest consciously. Methodist preaching of God's love constituted an interpretation of the transference that recognized its inappropriateness without attempting to trace its biographical origin. In providing access to repressed aggression, the negative aspects of Methodist repentance were cathartic and could be therapeutic.

Psychoanalysts since Freud (1937) have regarded the fear of imminent death as a manifest content that symbolizes unconscious anxieties of potentially varied origin. William of St. Thierry's theory that meditation on the passion aroused panic in meditators who had guilty consciences similarly regarded the manifest content as a symbolic manifestation of unconscious fears whose contents were otherwise. Psychoanalysts have debated whether death, considered as a cessation of experience, can be feared (Fenichel, 1945; Meyer, 1975); but a consensus agrees that death is feared primarily because death involves a loss of loving relationships. Jones (1944, p. 317) remarked: "Dread of death invariably proves clinically to be the expression of repressed death wishes against loved objects." Meditators on the passion manifestly desired Christ's death for the sake of their own souls' ransom. The meditations may be expected to have unconsciously stimulated the meditator's Oedipus complexes, causing the meditations to become vehicles for "repressed death wishes against the parents, with a consequent fear of retaliation" (Jones, 1944, p. 317). The unconscious fear of parental retaliation generated the manifest negativity of the transference onto God. Reacting to the knowledge of mortality as a statement of divine rejection, the ego enters an intrapsychic transference. It is as though in its self-focus, the ego concludes, "I am going to die because I am being abandoned. I must have been bad."

If we accept William's theory that crucifixion with Christ was a symptom of a guilty conscience, we may ask what in its content shifted self-focused guilty panic to become an interpersonal, relational guilt for which reparation could be made. What tipped the scales in favor of therapeutic change? Meditation on the passion was able to induce abreactive states, consistent with panic attacks that occur as part of the transference neuroses of psychoanalytic patients; but the medieval experience was able to resolve itself, moving from abreactive reliving of the panic to a cathartic remembering, as from a psychic distance. How did the medieval practice accomplish what the intervention of an analyst is needed to produce during a psychoanalysis?

Later medieval writers suggested that mystical death yielded to a positive contemplative experience upon the achievement of compassion. James of Milan asserted that consolation was contingent on compassion. In Middle English translation, he advised meditators: "thou strengthen thee in all that thou mayst for to have compassion of Christ's passion, overall bearing it in thy heart, for but if we can have compassion, we may not receive consolation" (Hilton, 1952, pp. 142–43). The medieval use of the expression "but if" had the sense of modern "unless." "But if [=unless] we can have compassion, we may not receive consolation." Hilton expressed the same opinion. "A person shall not commonly come to spiritual delight in the contemplation of Christ's divinity unless he first come in imagination by anguish and compassion for his humanity" (Hilton, 1991, p. 106).

What was at stake, I sugest, was how meditators understood Luke 23:34, "And Jesus said, 'Father, forgive them; for they know not what they do.'" Meditators' rage against the Jews and the Roman soldiers had been unforgiving. Now, with Jesus crucified and nearing death, meditators were required to consider Jesus' compassion. Meditators who adopted the perspectives of eyewitnesses cast themselves in the role of being recipients of Jesus' compassion, incurring gratitude to Jesus that might serve only to intensify a neurotic sense of unworthiness and anxiety. However, meditators who proceeded from the imagined perspective of Jesus cultivated a different emotional configuration. The fear of imagined death provided an opportunity for a guilty conscience to manifest fear of retaliation in the form of a fearful mystical death. This awakening of unconsious conscience through admission of its symbolism to consciousness was compounded through meditation on Jesus' compassion. When meditators attempted to have Christ-like compassion for others, the passion narrative encouraged them to shift from self-focus to relationality. The narrative provided the idea of compassion. Meditations were successful when they achieved compassion's immediate emotional experience. However momentarily, they were reformed in faith and in feeling. Upon achieving compassion, meditators ceased to be guilty of rage and hate, ceased to have unconscious cause to fear retaliation, and were additionally able to forgive themselves. Their self-forgiveness constituted permission to experience the euphoric ecstasy of a clear conscience, and resurrection followed.

The transition from guilty panic in the face of death to sorrowful compassion for humanity implied a reconciliation with conscience—in psychoanalytic terms, an integration of the superego within the ego. With repeated experience, momentary achievements of integration might be internalized as a permanent acquisition of the psyche. A limited integration with the id may also have been achieved. Approaching psychoanalysis from an existential perspective, Ernest Becker (1973) suggested that death, like sexuality, has the psychological function of locating the psyche in the human body, with all of its embarrassing, humbling, animal implications. The embodied nature of mystical death may be expected, among other effects, to have added importance to the experience of chastisement. The prospect of dying was not lightly to be ignored. Although the death was mystical and not physiological, its vividness as an imagined bodily experience aroused a depth of fear that merited serious attention.

RESURRECTION AS PLAY

A few medieval references to crucifixion with Christ mention acute fear, consistent with panic attacks. Others speak only of bitterness, agony, or suffering, as is consistent with the cross-cultural finding that with repeated experience, mystical death may cease to be terrifying and may instead be greeted with equanimity (Merkur, 1992, 1998a, 1999). Death never ceases to be realistically fearful, but the ego is able gradually to master the neurotic overlay. Winnicott (1989, pp. 92-93) maintained that the fear of death is a fear of something that has already happened, that it projects into the future a sense of catastrophe that occurred during infancy when the individual was too immature to comprehend a failure on the part of the mother as other than an annihilation of self. Winnicott's clinical advice, that the fear of death be interpreted as a past reality rather than a future prospect, occurs spontaneously during mystical death when people survive them. After experiencing panic during an intensely vivid imagination of dying, people alert from the experience with the realization that they are alive, that they have not died, that they have had vivid imaginations of dying, but have not been at risk of dying in reality. With repeated experience, self-observations of the idea of mortality cease to arouse the irrational fear that death is a rejection, abandonment, and punishment. Death becomes, only and simply, mortality, a cessation of fear.

Alerting from a mystical death is analogous to the interpretation of the transference in American ego psychology. An austere psychoanalytic frame is maintained until the patient enters a "regressive transference neurosis" (Stone, 1961; Greenson, 1967) that consists of sustained rage at the analyst. Although the analyst's actual behavior is the occasion of the rage (Gill, 1982), the patient's style of rage owes to precedents that go back to infancy and childhood. When the analyst interprets the rage as a transference from one or both parents onto the analyst, and the patient recognizes that the interpretation is at least partly valid, the patient also alerts from the rage, recognizes it as a reliving of past emotion, and conceptualizes the rage within the context of the child's understanding of its circumstances. Like alerting from a mystical death, achieving insight into a regressive transference neurosis involves a transition from relived emotion to self-reflection.

Because self-observation is a superego function (Freud, 1933), the transition from mystical death to awareness of its survival constitutes a shift from symbolism of repressed superego materials to the superego's conscious manifestation. Insight into the imaginary nature of mystical death serves as a point of access, the thin edge of a wedge by which the relational thinking of the superego gains access to consciousness and is able to engage the ego in an intrapsychic relationship. Because the experience of grace is an intrinsically relational process, the ego must open to relationality if it is to experience grace as such. The ego's need to open to relationality underlies Hilton's (1991) assertion, "A person shall not commonly come to spiritual delight in the contemplation of Christ's divinity unless he first comes in imagination by anguish and compassion for his humanity" (p. 106).

Importantly, awareness of having survived mystical death opens the experience to the possibility of being interpreted as a symbol. The circumstance parallels nocturnal dreams, which cannot ordinarily be submitted to interpretation until the dreamer wakes. Hilton's doctrine that the visual image of Jesus that is beheld during mystical death is a visual image of the meditator's soul, which is created in the image of God, explicitly treated mystical death as a symbolic event that occurs to the human soul. If the practice of meditation had not already fostered an understanding of metaphor, the experience of mystical death would do so. In this manner, meditators who had been unable to play with their religious ideas, were brought to a state of being able to play.

In the fourteenth century, Julian of Norwich had a vision of Christ crucified that she attributed to a deathly illness. Because the vision was known as
such during its occurrence, it was self-evidently metaphoric. Julian wrote:

> And suddenly it came into my mind that I ought to wish for the sec-
> ond wound, that our Lord, of his gift and of his grace, would fill my
> body full with recollection and feeling of his blessed Passion, as I had
> prayed before, for I wished that his pains might be my pains, with
> compassion which would lead to longing for God. So it seemed to me
> that I might with his grace have his wounds, as I had wished before;
> but in this I never wanted any bodily vision or any kind of revelation
> from God, but only the compassion which I thought a loving soul
> could have for our Lord Jesus, who for love was willing to become a
> mortal man. I desired to suffer with him, living in my mortal body, as
> God would give me grace. And at this, suddenly I saw the red blood
> trickling down from under the crown, all hot, flowing freely and copi-
> ously, a living stream, just as it seemed to me that it was at the time
> when the crown of thorns was thrust down upon his blessed head. Just
> so did he, both God and man, suffer for me. I perceived, truly and
> powerfully, that it was himself who showed this to me, without any
> intermediary; and then I said: Blessed be the Lord! This I said with a
> reverent intention and in a loud voice, and I was greatly astonished by
> this wonder and marvel, that he would so humbly be with a sinful
> creature living in this wretched flesh. I accepted it that at that time
> our Lord Jesus wanted, out of his courteous love, to show me comfort
> before my temptations began; for it seemed to me that I might well
> be tempted by devils, by God's permission and with his protection,
> before I died. With this sight of his blessed Passion and with his
> divinity, of which I speak as I understand, I saw that this was strength
> enough for me, yes, and for all living creatures who will be protected
> from all the devils of hell and from all their spiritual enemies.
>   And at the same time as I saw this corporeal sight, our Lord
> showed me a spiritual sight of his familiar love. I saw that he is to us
> everything which is good and comforting for our help. He is our
> clothing, for he is that love which wraps and enfolds us, embraces us
> and guides us, surrounds us for his love, which is so tender that he
> may never desert us. And so in this sight I saw truly that he is every-
> thing which is good, as I understand. (Julian, 1978, pp. 129–30)

With the realization that the envisioned image of Jesus was not Jesus, but
was instead a revelation shown to her by Jesus, Julian commenced thinking
relationally about Jesus. The visionary state immediately shifted from the mor-

bid images of the passion to euphoric images and ideas that, in another writer, might have been termed the resurrection. Jesus loved and comforted her. He embraced, guided and surrounded all things. From a psychoanalytic perspective, we may also speak of a manifestation of Julian's self-esteem, which is another superego function (Jacobson, 1964).

WORKING THROUGH

Through repeated experience, the momentary enhancement of self-esteem during a religious experience may gradually lead to an increased capacity for self-esteem. Feeling innocent similarly leads to forgiving self, ceasing to rage against self and others, and ending ambivalence toward Jesus. Idealization, against which split-off derogation is a reaction-formation, becomes less extreme and is internalized as an ego ideal that can be loved, cherished, honored, and otherwise engaged in a relationship. Becoming capable, as well, of less conflicted admiration of and faith in Jesus makes possible living up to Jesus' behavioral standard, and feeling in conformity with his sweetness.

CONCLUDING REFLECTIONS

Meditation on the passion may be conceptualized as a medieval form of guided imagery therapy. In a fashion that is consistent with Klein's and Winnicott's ideas about therapeutic progress, the passion narrative progresses from self-focus and splitting on the way to Golgotha, to interpersonal relationality on the cross. Therapeutic action presumably occurred when the passion narrative was internalized as a meditator's own experience. Splitting, with aggression against God being displaced against the Jews and the Roman soldiers, helped to circumvent the customary Christian denial of death and facilitated the emergence in consciousness of the fear of death. The arousal of negative emotions would not have been therapeutic when meditations proceeded from the perspective of an eyewitness; but mystical death both brought unconscious guilt to consciousness and precipitated self-reflection as the panic subsided abruptly. Meditation on compassion, as felt by Jesus in the passion narrative, then joined with self-reflection in order to integrate the superego's relational thinking within consciousness. The therapeutic action was consistent with the shift from murderous rage through guilt to remorse in the conversion legend of St. Paul. It was also consistent with insight into a regressive transference neurosis, as it might be produced in a self-analysis.

Chapter 6

The Death of Adam

The medieval achievement in spiritual direction that culminated in the work of Hilton may be measured against two narratives in *The Dialogues* that St. Gregory the Great wrote in 593, shortly after he became Pope. One is an episode from the legend of St. Benedict of Nursia (d. 550).

> The evil spirit recalled to his mind a woman he had once seen, and before he realized it his emotions were carrying him away. Almost overcome in the struggle, he was on the point of abandoning the lonely wilderness, when suddenly with the help of God's grace he came to himself.
>
> He then noticed a thick patch of nettles and briers next to him. Throwing his garment aside he flung himself into the sharp thorns and stinging nettles. There he rolled and tossed until his whole body was in pain and covered with blood. Yet, once he had conquered pleasure through suffering, his torn and bleeding skin served to drain the poison of temptation from his body. Before long, the pain that was burning his whole body had put out the fires of evil in his heart. It was by exchanging these two fires that he gained the victory over sin. So complete was his triumph that from then on, as he later told his disciples, he never experienced another temptation of this kind. (Gregory, 1959, p. 59–60)

In this narrative, virtue was achieved through a mastery of inner conflict. Benedict had been able, with God's grace, to recognize the intensity of his sexual desires. By inflicting severe pain on himself, he had been able to bring an end to his experience of desire. This particular incident was significant because it provided not only temporary respite from a particular sexual fantasy, but a permanent end to Benedict's experience of sexual desire.

Although asceticism has a broad range of wholesome and morbid uses, the scourging that Benedict inflicted on himself achieved its effects, I suggest, through self-traumatization. The self-scourging was not simply a distraction from a passing sexual fantasy. Gregory's tale implied that Benedict's self-scourging was a desperate enactment of guilt over having sexual desires. The self-punishment was so severe that Benedict lost consciousness of further sexual desire. However, the conflicted nature of his celibacy is indicated by the invention of his monastic rule, his limitation of human contacts to fellow monks, and his eventual abandonment of monastic life for "the wilderness he loved, to live alone with himself in the presence of his heavenly Father" (p. 62). Benedict's avoidance of spontaneity, women, and ultimately, men, attests to the unconscious continuation of his sexual desires. He needed to resort to increasingly severe measures in order to keep sexual desire from manifesting consciously. He was not able to experience "the presence of his heavenly Father" in a manner that he found satisfactory while living in community. Importantly, the inculcation of guilt through pain and deprivation to the point that a person betrays his or her authentic personhood in order to avoid the pain of further guilt, is well-known in recent history as the operative principle of brainwashing or thought reform (Lifton, 1956, 1961). It is an inculcation of a false conscience—what Fairbairn (1963) termed "the antilibidinal subject" as distinct from the true superego.

Gregory's *Dialogues* also narrated a second story of a permanent cessation of temptation. Its outcome was strikingly different:

> Finding himself much distressed as a young man by violent temptations of the flesh, Equitius turned with all the greater zeal to fervent prayer. One night while he was earnestly begging God for aid in this matter, he saw himself made a eunuch while an angel stood by. Through this vision he realized that all disturbances of the flesh had been taken away, and from that time on he was a complete stranger to temptations of this kind as though his body were no longer subject to the tendencies of human nature.
>
> Relying on this virtue, which God had helped him to acquire, he took upon himself the guidance of communities of women just as he had done of monks. Yet he warned his disciples to be distrustful of themselves and not to be too eager to follow his example, for they would be the cause of their own downfall in trying to do what God had not given them the power to do. (Gregory the Great, 1959, p. 16)

The narrative concerns an achievement of psychic integration with a celibate sexual orientation, which was the standard goal of personality change among medieval religious in Western Christianity. Equitius' distress over "violent temptations of the flesh" indicated that his celibacy was not a neurotic indifference to sexuality. He was far from apathetic, and his election of celibacy may be interpreted as comformance with a cultural ideal. The conformance may have involved a genuine integration of the psyche. Integration is defined by its type of change, not by its extent. It is axiomatic that a psychoanalyst can help a patient to become only as well-integrated as the analyst happens to be, because no analyst can think to say to others what the analyst cannot think to achieve for him- or herself. So too with the integrations historically achieved in different eras and cultures. Integration is not less real, however, for being only partial—psychic integration is always only partial.

Supporting this reading of Gregory's tale of Equitius is another narrative concerning Equitius' vocation. Equitius had evidently been pursuing authenticity for some time prior to his integration of celibacy. Concerning his vocation, Gregory reported Equitius as saying:

'One night a young man of radiant beauty appeared to me in a vision and placed a lancet on my tongue and said, "Behold, I have put my words in your mouth. Go forth and preach." Since that day I could not be silent about God even if I so wished.' (Gregory the Great, 1959, p. 19)

For Gregory, the event was to be accepted at face value. God, or perhaps an angel, appeared to Equitius and commanded him to preach. From a psychoanalytic perspective, we may understand the vision as a manifestation of a personal ideal that was integral to Equitius' conscience. His sense of authenticity demanded preaching as a matter of self-expression. He was motivated not primarily by guilt, or duty, or compassion, but by the desire to be himself. His loss of sexual temptation was equally consistent with his authenticity. It was not a product of traumatizing self-punishment. It was an interior psychological development signalled to consciousness in the form of a vision.

For Gregory, however, both the narratives of Benedict and Equitius concerned a single phenomenon. In Gregory's presentation what was at stake theologically was an end to temptation. How it was achieved was unimportant. Both men's stories were plainly and simply miracles. It was impossible within Gregory's worldview to interpret Equitius' vision as an event that symbolized change within Equitius' soul. For Gregory, there was nothing symbolic about Equitius' vision. The angel that Equitius beheld protected him from demonic sendings of temptation. Mystical theology had to undergo considerable development before Hilton could entertain the concept that a vision of Christ crucified was not an interior perception of Christ, but was instead a mental image within a meditator's soul that might, with God's grace, induce a change, not in the behavior of demons, but exclusively of the soul's capacity for faith and feeling.

THE EARLY MEDIEVAL REJECTION OF VISIONS

The Latin monastic tradition had been deeply impressed by the fourth-century teachings of Evagrius Ponticus (345–399), a Desert Father who had had the benefit of training as a theologian. Among his many contributions to mystical theology, Evagrius had forbidden the practice of visualization. In his *Chapters on Prayer*, Evagrius (1981) wrote: "Do not by any means strive to fashion some image or visualize some form at the time of prayer" (p. 74). Evagrius feared being corrupted by demonic visions. "See to it that the evil demons do not lead you astray by means of some vision" (p. 71). Evagrius did not differentiate demonic and angelic visions. He suggested that what appear to be angels may be demons who have disguised themselves as angels:

> It is proper that you be advised about another ruse. The demons divide up into two groups for a time, and when they see you calling out for help against the one group the others make their appearance under the form of angels who drive away the first group. They have in mind to deceive you into believing that they are holy angels in all truth. (p. 71)

Taken for granted in this teaching was the belief that visions are accurate perceptions of objectively existing spiritual beings. Visions were not considered to be symbolic representations of spiritual truths by means of mental images. Consistent with Evagrius' distrust of visions was his limitation of mysticism to physical actions and conceptual experiences. "Christianity is the dogma of Christ our Savior," he wrote. "It is composed of *praktike*, of the contemplation of the physical world, and of the contemplation of God" (p. 15).

A similar doctrine was expressed in a tale about St. Anthony that was included in the *Apophthegmata Patrum*, "Sayings of the Fathers," a late sixth-century collection of traditions about desert monks from the early fourth century and onward:

> Some brothers came to find Abba Anthony to tell him about the visions they were having, and to find out from him if they were true or if they came from the demons. They had a donkey which died on the way. When they reached the place where the old man was, he said to them before they could ask him anything, 'How was it that the little donkey died on the way here?' They said, 'How do you know about

that, Father?' And he told them, 'The demons shewed me what happened.' So they said, 'That was what we came to question you about, for fear we were being deceived, for we have visions which often turn out to be true.' Thus the old man convinced them, by the example of the donkey, that their visions came from the demons. (Ward, 1975, p. 3)

When demons chose to tell the truth, visions were truthful; but because visions were sent by demons they were never to be trusted.

Benedict (d. 550) recommended the *Apophthegmata* in the final chapter of his *Rule* (Fry, 1982, p. 95). He also recommended the writings of John Cassian (c. 360-after 430), who had been taught mysticism by the Greek-speaking Evagrius Ponticus. Cassian, who wrote in Latin, recommended the ceaseless repetition of the prayer, "O God, incline unto my aid; O Lord, make haste to help me," among other reasons, as an antidote to visions of unclean spirits. This technique of prayer countered "wandering thoughts . . . foolish fantasies" and memories, and it resulted in "spiritual thoughts . . . due to a sudden illumination from the Lord" (Cassian, 1997, pp. 381–82; see also Chadwick, 1968, pp. 105–7). Through the *Apophthegmata* and Cassian's writings, a rejection of visions was formative of the Latin monastic tradition.

The rejection of visions was integral to the promotion of the view, championed by Evagrius and Cassian among others, that the image and likeness of God in Genesis 1:26 were to be understood "not according to the lowly sound of the letter but in a spiritual way" (Cassian, 1997, p. 372). Cassian related the following incident that occurred when an elderly monk in the Egyptian desert was told of the prohibition of anthropomorphism by his deacon Photinus. The monk attempted to pray in the manner he had been instructed:

> But the old man got so confused in his mind during the prayers, when he realized that the anthropomorphic image of the Godhead which he had always pictured to himself while praying had been banished from his heart, that he suddenly broke into the bitterest and heavy sobbing and, throwing himself to the ground with a loud groan, cried out: "Woe is me, wretch that I am! They have taken my God from me, and I have no one to lay hold of, nor do I know whom I should adore or address." (Cassian, 1997, p. 373)

Because anthropomorphism was a theological error, its prohibition implied that entertaining a mental image of God in human form was a fallacy. Knowingly praying to a fallacy was not only pointless, but impious. However, because the old monk knew no other way to pray, he found himself unable to contact his God (Carruthers, 1998, p. 71). The implication for visionary practice is equally notable. Should a mental image develop into a passively received vision, its failure to pertain to God meant the vision had necessarily to be demonic.

Throughout the Middle Ages, mental images continued to be cultivated under the terms "recollection" and "meditation," for the purposes of mnemonics, thoughtful reasoning, and rhetorical composition (Carruthers, 1998, pp. 7–170). Because imagination was regarded as a clothing of ideas in images supplied by memories of sense perceptions, the meditations and visualizations were regarded as nonmystical recollections of memory and reasoning. Verbal thinking and mental imaging were understood to be human acts that were within the natural power of human will. Contemplation and vision were instead regarded as manifestations of divine grace. The distinction between the two was ontological. Voluntary mental imagining, visualization, could not cause divine grace. Experiences that mental imagining could cause were necessarily not grace. Conversely, before a visionary experience could be claimed to be a divine grace, there had to be compelling reason to believe that it illumined the mind with "divine revelation" that was either "internally pictured in the imagination" or "perceived internally through imagination due to God's action" (Aquinas, *Summa Contra Gentiles* III, ii, Ch 154, 4). "The gift of grace surpasses every capacity of created nature, since it is nothing other than a certain participation in the divine nature" (Aquinas, *Summa Theologiae*, 1a2ae. 112, 1). Consider, for example, a vision seen by Benedict, as chronicled in Gregory's *Dialogues*:

> Long before the night office began, the man of God was standing at his window, where he watched and prayed while the rest were still asleep. In the dead of night he suddenly beheld a flood of light shining down from above more brilliant than the sun, and with it every trace of darkness cleared away. Another remarkable sight followed. According to his own description, the whole world was gathered up before his eyes in what appeared to be a single ray of light. As he gazed at all this dazzling display, he saw the soul of Germanus, the Bishop of Capua, being carried by angels up to heaven in a ball of fire. (Gregory, 1959, p. 105)

Benedict was employing mental images in a customary and routine fashion during his reflections. For rhetorical purposes, the mental images were called "darkness" that his vision was said to vanquish (Carruthers, 1998, p. 192). Gregory's rhetoric stressed the categorical contrast between the darkness, which was a natural part of the night that was Benedict's soul, and the visionary light from on high. Any development from the one to the other would have precluded the possibility that Benedict's vision of the world's union was a grace of God.

The fear of being misled by visions was given a theological rationale by Cassian's contemporary, Augustine of Hippo (354–430). In Book Twelve, of *The Literal Meaning of Genesis*, Augustine divided visions into three categories. The visions differed according to the faculty of the soul that apprehended them:

> We experience three kinds of vision: one through the eyes, by which we see the letters; a second through the spirit, by which we think of our neighbor even when he is absent; and a third through an intuition of the mind, by which we see and understand love itself. (Augustine, 1982, p. 185)

Augustine named the three types of vision corporeal, spiritual, and intellectual, respectively (see also: Tobin, 1995, pp. 42–48).

Unlike the broad current use of the term "spiritual," Augustine defined spiritual visions in a technical fashion that was consistent with the Neoplatonic concept of imagination. "The word spirit is taken . . . in the sense of a power of the soul inferior to the mind, wherein likenesses of corporeal objects are produced" (Augustine, 1982, p. 189). By *spiritus*, Augustine was translating the Greek *pneuma*, a term that Neoplatonists used to designate ether, the ostensible substance of star light. Neoplatonists believed that the soul was purely intellectual, but possessed an ethereal or pneumatic vehicle that could be beheld by the imaginative faculty (Finamore, 1985; Blumenthal, 1992). Augustine explained that spiritual visions might disclose "true images, representing the bodies that we have seen and still hold in memory, or fictitious images, fashioned by the power of thought" (p. 186). In the middle ages, when the term "spiritual" regularly referred to the Holy Spirit, which is perceived exclusively by the intellect, what Augustine had called a spiritual vision was instead called interior or imaginative.

Because Augustine accepted Neoplatonism's hierarchic ranking of the faculties of the soul, he acknowledged that the mind advanced from corporeal perception, to spiritual image-making that was based on memory, to intellectual understandings of the images as signs or, as we might say, metaphors (Augustine, 1982, pp. 191–93). In contrast, however, with the mind's natural progression from perceptions to memories to abstractions, there were no links by which a mystic proceeded from corporeal, to spiritual, and then to intellectual visions (McGinn, 1991, p. 261). For Augustine, each category of experience was autonomous. Visions occurred "when the soul is carried off to objects of vision" that were variously corporeal, spiritual, or intellectual (p. 216). Corporeal, spiritual, and intellectual visions beheld phenomena that were corporeal, spiritual, and intellectual, respectively. In the case of spiritual—that is, imaginative—visions, "the revelation must come only from some spirit"

(Augustine, 1982, p. 295). Intellectual visions were similarly dependent on intelligible phenomena, which is to say, abstract concepts. "How else can the intellect itself be seen except by intellection?" (p. 213).

In *The City of God*, Augustine discussed techniques for inducing spiritual visions in the course of a polemic against Porphyry (c. 232–304), a pagan Neoplatonist who advocated visualization alongside ablutions, sacrifices, and ritual invocations collectively termed "theurgy." Like Christians, theurgists faulted magic because it claimed to force the gods. Theurgists performed what they regarded as divinely ordained rites in order to submit to the gods' will and await their grace (Hadot, 2002, 170–71). Augustine explained that Porphyry "declares that it [theurgy] is useful as a means of purifying one part of the soul: not, indeed, the intellectual part, which perceives the truth of intelligible things which have no bodily likenesses, but the spiritual part, whereby we receive the images of corporeal things. This part, he says, is made fit and suitable for the reception of spirits and angels, and for seeing the gods, by certain theurgic consecrations which are called mysteries" (Augustine, 1998, p. 404). Augustine rejected theurgy because, in his view, the soul needs no special preparation for one type of vision as distinct from the others:

> We need not seek one purification for the part which Porphyry calls intellectual, and another for the part he calls spiritual, and another for the body itself; for our most true and mighty Purifier and Saviour took upon Himself the whole of human nature. (p. 446)

As well, whatever a spiritual vision might reveal to the soul's imaginative faculty could not be God. "The aspect under which God is seen even though He is by nature invisible is not the same thing as God Himself. It is, however, He Himself Who is seen under that bodily aspect" (pp. 411–12).

Not only did Augustine think visualization pointless and vain, but he was generally pessimistic about spiritual visions. Intellectual visions were reliable to the extent that they were coherent or rational.: "By means of corporeal vision as well as by means of the images of corporeal objects revealed in the spirit, good spirits instruct men and evil spirits deceive them. But there is no deception in intellectual vision; for either a person does not understand . . . or he does understand, and then his vision is necessarily true" (Augustine, 1982, p. 197). Arguing by inference from St. Paul's critique of the incoherence of speaking in tongues (1 Cor 14:1–12), Augustine devalued spiritual visions as a class (Augustine, 1982, pp. 188–89):

> Those to whom signs were manifested in the spirit by means of certain likenesses of corporeal objects had not yet the gift of prophecy, unless the mind had performed its function, in order that the signs

might be understood; and the man who interpreted what another had seen was more a prophet than the man who had seen. . . . And so Joseph, who understood the meaning of the seven ears of corn and the seven kind, was more a prophet than Pharaoh, who saw them in a dream; for Pharaoh saw only a form impressed upon his spirit, whereas Joseph understood through a light given to his mind. (p. 189)

Augustine insisted that Paul's claim of having been "caught up to the third heaven" referred allegorically to the third type of vision, intellectual vision (p. 219). He was not prepared to accept the plain meaning of Paul's language, which had reported a spiritual vision. The allegorization of the language of ascension had become normative by Augustine's period (Jonas, 1969; Daniélou, 1973, pp. 447–500). Mystics, whose visions were intellectual, continued to use language derived from early Christian apocalypses in which visionaries had flown into the sky, toured heaven, and met with God seated on his throne. For example, Evagrius Ponticus (1981) wrote, "Prayer is an ascent of the spirit to God" (p. 60). Used in reference to intellectual experiences, the language of ascension was metaphoric.

In limiting the use he made of Neoplatonism, Augustine eliminated the Hellenistic idea that the mystic way accomplished a series of ontological changes as the mystic ascended from hypostasis to hypostasis. In Neoplatonism, Gnosticism, and Hermetism, the soul began embodied, shed its material body to become an ethereal or other spiritual body, and finally, shed its spiritual body in order to become mind or intellect alone. In Augustine's presentation, no such transformations occurred. A mystic stayed in the perceptible world, ascended nowhere, and underwent no ontological change. Just as the soul's corporeal senses provided perceptions of physical objects, the soul's spiritual faculty apprehended spiritual beings, and the soul's intellect contemplated intelligibles. Like different colors of light, sensibles, imaginables, and intelligibles were present in creation simultaneously.

Gregory the Great (540?–604) further simplified the Latin theological scheme. An encyclopedic collection of miracles that occurred in the Italian Christian community, his *Dialogues* boast of a great many visions. These visions were regularly interpreted as paranormal events: There were prophecies that came true (p. 228); visions of souls ascending to heaven at death, often in the accompaniment of angels (pp. 105, 108, 201, 203, 228); visions of a soul being released from purgatory (p. 269); visions of prophets (p. 233); saints (pp. 156–57, 186, 204–5, 211); God (p. 210); Mary (p. 211–12); heaven (pp. 221–23, 241); demons (pp. 74–75, 121, 245–46); and hell (p. 241).

Most of the visions Gregory reported occurred when peope were severely ill (p. 260), as they were about to die (pp. 204, 210–12, 221–23, 233, 235, 245–6, 259–60), or after they had died and returned to life (pp. 50–51, 239)—in modern terms, during delirium or near death experiences. Comparatively few experiences that involved a voluntary component met Gregory's criterion for inclusion as visions. He allowed that Benedict had gone "in spirit to his sleeping brethren" so that they saw his soul in a dream (pp. 90–91). Gregory also acknowledged that "it was with spiritual vision, purified by acts of faith and abundant prayers, that many of our people were able repeatedly to observe souls leaving the body" (p. 200). The visions remained spiritual perceptions of supernatural realities—what we today call extrasensory perceptions. Similarly, Gregory believed that when "a man of flesh and blood saw an object which was physically real to him," we are to "understand that the soul is transported spiritually" (p. 235).

Gregory regarded anxiety as a normal response to holy visions. He related that once, after the Pope summoned Equitius, on "the very night he had set out from Rome, the Pope had been terrified in a vision for having summoned the man of God" (Gregory, 1959, p. 22). Gregory accounted for the anxiety by reference to Scripture.

> Have you forgotten the words of the Prophet Daniel, who trembled at the sight of his mighty and terrifying vision? 'I became weak,' he said, 'and was sick for some days.' The flesh is overwhelmed by the things of the spirit. Sometimes, therefore, when the mind is allowed to see beyond its human powers, the body cannot but grow weak, because the task imposed is more than it can endure. (p. 157)

Gregory was aware that in some cases visions were symbolic, but they remained paranormal all the same. He wrote: "We arrive at a true understanding through images. For example, the just were seen passing over a bridge to a beautiful meadow, because the road that leads to eternal life is narrow" (p. 242). Gregory held that nightly visions or dreams were to be trusted if they were demonstrably miraculous, but otherwise not.

> Dreams come to the soul in six ways. They are generated either by a full stomach or by an empty one, or by illusions, or by our thoughts combined with illusions, or by revelations, or by our thoughts combined with revelations. (p. 261)

Dreams and visions that were illusions, were produced by the Devil. Divination was an instance of demonic illusions combined with human thoughts; revelations were instanced by Scripture (p. 261). This last category was as close as Gregory came to a discussion of visualization:

> If at times dreams did not proceed from the thoughts in our minds as well as from revelation, the Prophet Daniel, in interpreting the dream

of Nabuchodonosor, would not have started on the basis of a thought, saying, 'Thou, O king, didst begin to think in thy bed what should come to pass hereafter: and he that reveals mysteries showed thee what shall come to pass." And a little later, 'Thou O king, sawest, and behold there was as it were a great statue: this statue, which was great and high, all of stature, stood before thee,' and so on. Daniel, therefore, in reverently indicating that the dream was to be fulfilled and in telling from what thoughts it arose, shows clearly that dreams often rise from our thoughts and from revelation. (p. 262)

Although Gregory acknowledged the prophetic and miraculous character of visions, he endorsed the monastic tradition of avoiding their cultivation:

Seeing, then, that dreams may arise from such a variety of causes, one ought to be very reluctant to put one's faith in them, since it is hard to tell from what source they come. The saints, however, can distinguish true revelations from the voices and images of illusions through an inner sensitivity. They can always recognize when they receive communications from the good Spirit and when they are face to face with illusions. (p. 262)

Gregory's approach to visions dominated the monastic tradition during the early middle ages, leading to a comparative neglect of Augustine's greater psychological sophistication until its twelfth century revival. Rather than to divide visions among three Neoplatonic categories, Gregory contrasted the corporeal and exterior with the spiritual and interior (Markus, 1969, p. 208). His scheme eradicated the differences among types of interior or spiritual experience. Because both were interior, the imagistic experiences that Augustine had called spiritual were categorized together with intellectual experiences. For example, the vision of an angel was placed on the same theological footing as a conceptual contemplation of divine unity. Both were considered veridical. The vision was not appreciated in the Neoplatonic manner, endorsed by Augustine, as a fitting of sense-based images to the abstract idea of an invisible power. Within Gregory's theology, there was no possibility of interpreting mental imagery as imaginative. Belief was placed "in a densely incorporeal population that could be glimpsed under special circumstances" (Erickson, 1976, p. 29). Images were either veridical or demonic. There was no category for the psychological.

Gregory's precedent dominated Latin vision literature from the sixth through the eleventh centuries. The visions were regularly claimed to be spontaneous and involuntary. They were generally portrayed as unique, protracted experiences, usually of the visionary's transport to heaven or to hell. In many cases, visions were presented without any explanation as to how they had occurred (Adomnán, 1995); implicitly they were wholly gifts of grace. In other cases, visions were said to have been experienced by people who had died and revived (Patch, 1950, pp. 96–97, 100–1, 123; Gardiner, 1989, pp. 47, 48, 57, 152; Zaleski, 1987), been ill (Patch, 1950, pp. 99, 110, 112, 117, 118; Gardiner, 1989, pp. 51, 198–99), or been asleep (Patch, 1950, pp. 103, 109–10, 121, 124; Gardiner, 1989, pp. 129, 220; de Nie, 1987; see also: Hanson, 1980). These narrative devices were not accidental. In 824, the Benedictine abbot Heito of Reichenau composed *Wetti's Vision*, which reported the deathbed visions of a monk named Wetti. In its references to the monk's activities at prayer, public reading, nocturnal meditations, and so forth, the text makes abundant references to practices of recollection that presumably involved visualizations (Carruthers, 1998, pp. 79–83); but the three visions in the text are portrayed as near death experiences mediated by an angel (Gardiner, 1989, pp. 66, 67–68, 69). Again, the Welsh poems of the prophet Myrddin, some of which date to the ninth century, relate that he acquired the power of prophecy upon going mad during a battle (Jarman, 1959, pp. 20–21). Early medieval audiences would accept a portrait of posttraumatic stress disorder; they were not prepared to associate visionary experiences with visualization practices. Contemplative states and meditative practices differed categorically.

The Revival of Interest in Visions

The Western Christian attitude toward visions began to change in the twelfth century when several writers discussed visions that were individually brief, and occurred to single visionaries on several or many occasions (Dinzelbacher, 1981); several mystics became famous for their visions. However, the practice remained firmly in place of claiming that visions were spontaneous and involuntary gifts of grace. Rupert of Deutz claimed visions during light sleep (McGinn, 1994, p. 329). Hildegard of Bingen claimed waking visions from age three onward; she also mentioned her lifelong suffering of illnesses (McGinn, 1994, p. 334). The creative inspirations that Joachim of Fiore interpreted as intellectual visions, sometimes took form as figurative mental images (*figurae*) or imaginative visions; Joachim emphasized their sudden, revelatory character and unanticipated content (McGinn, 1994, p. 338).

As time passed, the experience of visions was routinized. Although some visionaries claimed their visions occurred during sleep or illness (De Gank, 1991, pp. 179, 201, 275; Julian, 1978, pp. 127–28), thirteenth- and fourteenth-century visionaries claimed with increasing frequency that they prayed or meditated on topics of their choice. In some cases, they formulated a question that they put directly to God. God then responded by removing them from the world of the senses and showing them visions (Mechthild, 1953, pp. 27, 32–33, 45, 58; Angela, 1993, pp. 130, 145, 169, 175, 180, 185, 186, 209, 245; Gertrude, 1993, pp. 48–49; Suso, 1989, p. 99). McGinn (1998) remarked that "these experiences tended to be repeatable apparitions consciously prepared for and expected." Nevertheless, the mystics' writings discussed imagery only as passive experiences of "revelation in pictorial form" (p. 27).

Consider, for example, the following account of the visions of St. Birgitta of Sweden (c. 1303–1373):

> The first divine revelations were made to Lady Birgitta not in sleep but while she was awake and at prayer, with her body remaining alive in its vigor, but while she was caught up from her bodily senses in ecstasy and in visions, either spiritual or imaginary, with the coming of a vision or a supernatural and divine illumination of her intellect, for she saw and heard spiritual things and felt them in spirit. Indeed, in the manner mentioned, she saw and heard corporeal images and similitudes; in fact, in her heart she felt something, as it were, alive, which moved more actively and more fervently in response to greater inflammations and infusions, but less when the infusions were less. Many times, indeed, the movement in her heart was so vehement that motion could be seen and felt even on the outside. (Birgitta, 1990, p. 78)

Medieval readers assumed that Birgitta's prayers were conducted in the customary manner—with mental images to enhance them. The *Life of Blessed Birgitta* emphasized the tokens of the authenticity of her visions. They were not dreams of sleep; they came while she was at prayer, and she did not collapse in a faint. Her body remained in its posture of prayer. However, she was oblivious to the world of sense perception when her mind was occupied with spiritual things, that is, with visions that were imaginative rather than intellectual. Birgitta sometimes saw and heard corporeal images and similitudes. Their distinction from sense perceptions was disclosed partly by their contents, but more importantly by involuntary motions of her heart, whose intensity varied with the visions. These involuntary motions were sometimes apparent to other people in the room with Birgitta, who watched her body while she was in ecstasy.

This account, like scores of others in medieval literature, was at pains to exclude the idea that visualizations during prayer induced visions that were subsequently experienced. Reports consistently weighted the distinction between the mystics' mental activities at prayer and their mental passivity following the *ligatura* or binding of the senses. What the mystics actively did, and what was done to them while they were passive, were emphatically distinct in their theologies.

To medieval thought, a visualization had no more influence on the subse-quent occurrence of a vision than a sight perception might have. Consider the following account by Gertrude of Helfta concerning:

> ... a remarkable prodigy which Thou didst show me in the image of Thy crucifixion. After I had received the Sacrament of life, and had retired to the place where I pray, it seemed to me that I saw a ray of light like an arrow coming forth from the wound of the right side of the crucifix, which was in an elevated place, and it continued, as it were, to advance and retire for some time, sweetly attracting my cold affections. (Petroff, 1986, p. 226)

Here, a vision of a ray of light emerged from a sight perception of a cru-cifix on the wall of Gertrude's place of prayer. A vision that emerged from a visualization was similarly categorically different. Visions were supernatural; they were passively received gifts of grace. Mental images, no different than sight perceptions, were voluntary, but they were wholly natural.

Bonaventure's biography of Francis carefully observed the medieval understanding of the supernaturalism of visions. In the *Legenda major*, Bonaventure wrote:

> On a certain morning about the feast of the Exaltation of the Cross, while Francis was praying on the mountainside, he saw a Seraph with six fiery and shining wings descend from the height of heaven. And when in swift flight the Seraph had reached a spot in the air near the man of God, there appeared between the wings the figure of a man crucified, with his hands and feet extended in the form of a cross and fastened to a cross. (Bonaventure, 1978, pp. 304-5)

In recounting the Seraphic vision of Francis, Bonaventure observed the same theological distinctions that Gregory the Great had employed in report-ing Benedict's vision six centuries earlier. According to *The Mind's Journey*, Francis had been engaging in meditation on the passion when he beheld a vision of a Seraph (Bonaventure, 1978, pp. 111–12). Presumably because the *Legenda major* was addressed to laity rather than to fellow contemplatives, Bonaventure did not explain that Francis had been actively imagining a man on a cross when he beheld the Seraph. He simply presented the vision as rad-ically different from the praying that Francis had been doing at the time.

Later, when the wings of the Seraph opened and "the figure of a man cru-cified" was revealed between them, Bonaventure did not refer to the man as Jesus or Christ because he knew that the image was a product of Francis's med-itation. Only the image of the seraph had the theological status of a vision. The

image of the crucified man had been produced through meditation and signified Francis himself. Bonaventure offered little discussion of Francis' meditation on the passion because it was merely a meditation. What was important
theologically was the vision of the Seraph. Francis had made no effort to visualize a Seraph. The image of a Seraph came to him unbidden. Its appearance
was an act of grace, a vision, that changed and augmented the mental imagery
that he had been visualizing.

A rare exception to the categorical distinction between visualizations and
visions indicates its importance to medieval mystics. Mechthild of Magdeburg
(1210–1297), who lapsed into trances daily beginning at the age of twelve,
once happened to pray using a mental image of her body as the prison of her
soul. This image then developed into a vision when a noble maid, attended by
handmaidens, entered the house and illuminated it (Mechthild, 1953, p. 245).
This rare report of meditative visualization furnishing images that were carried
over into an imaginative vision apparently pertained to an accidental occurrence. Mechthild insisted that "God Himself is my witness that I never consciously asked Him to give me the things [visions, and so forth] of which I
have written" (pp. 94–95).

From a modern perspective, we may conclude that the medieval visionaries relied extensively on unwitting autosuggestions (Arbman, 1963–68–70).
Their prayers and meditations were performed in conventional manners that
cultivated mental images as mnemonic and rhetorical adornment for prayers
and meditations that were verbal. In contrast with the usual practice of meditation, which led to a state of reverie whose imaginative character was generally self-evident, the medieval visionaries experienced what seemed to them to
be visions because they combined their meditations with dissociative states. By
désagrégation (dissociation), Pierre Janet referred to a splitting of consciousness
into a dual consciousness (*double conscience*) whose portions are not associated
or integrated with each other. The term was initially applied to hypnosis and
hysteria. When Freud (1894) introduced the concept of repression, he stressed
that dissociation is not a cause, but an effect, and always additionally involves
repressed materials that are unconscious. Due to the recent prominence of
multiple personality disorder and false memory syndrome—which is to say,
culturally fashionable forms of hysteria and hypnosis, respectively—the term
"dissociation" has returned to popularity. The term remains generic. Dissociative states may arise spontaneously as symptoms of physical illness or hysteria
(Lynn & Rhue, 1994; Showalter, 1997; Brenner, 2001). In other cases, they
may be cultivated through self-hypnotic techniques.

As the term "dissociation" is relevant to Christian mysticism, it may be
applied to the subjective experience of the detachment of consciousness from
part or all of its normal functions. Mystical theologians traditionally identified
the onset of the *ligatura* (binding), or *suspensio* (suspension), of sense perception

as marking a transition from active, voluntary thinking to passively received experiences of infused contemplation that they regarded as gifts of grace. Modern psychological research has established, however, that dissociation, which is an incrementally increasing process, typically begins to inhibit the sense of agency (will), reality testing, motor behavior, imagination, and thinking prior to having a subjectively noticeable impact on proprioception and sense perception. Not only are these several normal functions of consciousness lost to increasing extents as dissociation increases, but the repressed materials return to consciousness as involuntary automatisms of thought, imagery, behavior, and so forth (Merkur, 1984). Well before the *ligatura*, active voluntary mentation can, through dissociation, seem subjectively to be passively received inspirations that are indistinguishable from inspirations that originate unconsciously. During normal waking consciousness, active voluntary thinking is ordinarily self-evidently different from unconscious inspiration; but the repression of the sense of agency, together with the selective inhibition of reality-testing (Shor, 1959), can cause the apparent phenomenological difference to disappear when active thinking is dissociated. Whether unconscious inspirations are to be explained in naturalistic and/or theological terms, for example, as creative thoughts that are facilitated by grace, unconscious inspirations are easily confused with dissociated mentation during dissociated states.

The traditional assumption that the *ligatura* was a reliable index of infused contemplations was psychologically naive. Lacking concepts of unconscious determinism and the return of the repressed, theologians traditionally considered contemplations to be infusions of operative grace; but psychoanalytic theory instead would suggest an analogy with dreams. Dreams use conscious materials, often pertaining to events during the previous day, in unconscious thinking, where the previously conscious materials undergo dreamwork that converts them into the manifest contents of dreams. Mystical and visionary states may access aspects of the unconscious that are not ordinarily available to nocturnal dreams; but divine grace has no greater role to play in mystical and visionary states than it has in nocturnal dreams. Contemplations that coincide with the *ligatura* may involve *cooperative* grace, "in which our mind is both a mover and is moved, [and] the operation is attributed not only to God but also to the soul" (Aquinas, *Summa Theologiae*, 1a2ae. 111,2); but they do not consist of *operative* grace that is attributable exclusively to God.

At the same time, I see no reason to doubt the good faith of the visionary mystics of the late Middle Ages. Unlike Francis, the visionaries did not behold visions at the same time as the mental images or figures on which they were meditating; they had no basis for telling the two apart. Prior to their visions, they meditated in the conventional, nonmystical manner that included the picturing of mental images. They did not acknowledge that their prayers and meditations induced their visions. They were either naively unaware that their practices functioned as autosuggestions of the visions that followed, or in deference to Holy Mother Church they did not permit themselves to become aware of the connection. To have done so would have been to admit to engaging in theurgy, which was illicit. By 1300, a few individuals had come to recognize that their visualizations induced their visions, and they made bold to boast of their engagement in theurgy. They were promptly marginalized by the Church, while the mainline of Catholic visionaries trusted naively to the *ligatura* to prevent their visualizations from determining the contents of their visions.

Late medieval mystics understandably reported a great many visions without discussing their significance. A text such as *The Showings* of Julian of Norwich (1978), which elaborated on the theological implications of the imagery in Julian's visions, was decidedly rare. Most visionaries hesitated to make theological claims beyond the fact of having had visions. "In the intimate and subjective visions of late medieval nuns, the visions serve as a stamp of personal sanctity, confirmation of a privileged relationship with the loving Savior and Bridegroom" (Hamburger, 1989, p. 180). When the occurrence of a vision was treated as the token of Divine favor, theological unpacking of the vision's details was unimportant, and potentially embarrassing questions did not have to be asked.

Under the circumstances, the revival of interest in visions had no ready categories for the discussion of meditation on the passion. The meditations did not induce dissociative states. There was no *ligatura*. However, Latin Christianity had so defined contemplation that visualization had either to be meditative or theurgical. Meditation was within the scope of the soul's natural powers, theurgy was an activity of demons. What was one to make of meditations that were patently unitive and Christological?

PSEUDO-DIONYSIUS'S ECSTATIC ITINERARY

The solution to the theological dilemma was developed, I suggest, chiefly by Bernard of Clairvaux and Bonaventure, the two most important authorities on Latin mysticism in the High Middle Ages. They were inspired, however, by the formulations of the pseudonymous, Greek-writing, Syrian author of the early sixth century who signed himself Dionysius the Areopagite and claimed to be a contemporary of Paul. John Scotus Eriugena had translated pseudo-Dionysius into Latin in the ninth century; and interest in both pseudo-Dionysius (Knowles, 1975; McGinn, 1976) and Eriugena (Jeauneau, 1987) was revived in the twelfth century by Hugh of St. Victor and others. As St. Denis, pseudo-Dionysius was the patron saint of France. The first of all Gothic cathedrals, the royal sanctuary of St. Denis, was dedicated to him by Abbot Suger in 1144.

Latin authors of the twelfth century thoroughly revised what they borrowed from pseudo-Dionysius in order to subordinate his views to the formulations of Augustine. Although pseudo-Dionysius' texts were used with caution, they remained accessible in translation within the Latin world. They were valued particularly for their conceptions of celestial hierarchy, negative theology, and the symbolic significance of positive imagery. They were also important for introducing Christianity to the division of the mystic path into three stages (Nygren, 1953, pp. 573–74) that had originated with the Neoplatonist Proclus (1954). Latin authors ignored the second of his three stages of contemplation, because it involved a practice of visualization that they considered theurgical and illicit. However, his positive attitude toward mental imaging was happily applied to the practice of meditation by Bernard of Clairvaux, Hugh and Richard of St. Victor, and many others. In this manner, pseudo-Dionysius, whose mystical authority was second to none in the Eastern Church, also became a towering presence in the history of Latin Christianity (Knowles, 1975).

Let us examine the ecstatic itinerary that any medieval scholar might read in Latin translation, and yet might not fully discuss, much less endorse. In pseudo-Dionysius' system of Christian Neoplatonism, the three stages of purification, illumination, and perfection occurred and recurred at multiple levels of being. "The beatitude of God. . . . is full of a continuous light [that] . . . is purifying, illuminating, and perfecting; or rather it is itself purification, illumination, and perfection" (Pseudo-Dionysius, 1987, p. 155). Mirroring the triplicity of divine light, there were perfect angels above illuminated ones, and illuminated angels above purified ones. Among ecclesiastics, hierarchs, monks, and deacons were perfect, illuminated, and purified, respectively (pp. 238, 248). Pseudo-Dionysius also advocated Proclus' concept of emanations that are horizontal within an ontic rank, and not only vertical from one hypostasis to the next. Each rank of angels and ecclesiastics was itself purified, illuminated, and perfected (pp. 165, 167, 178, 238); and the sacramental rites of the Church were symbols variously of purification, illumination, and perfection (pp. 235–36).

For pseudo-Dionysius, purification was an elimination of evil (p. 204), a "drawing . . . away from all dalliance with what is evil" (p. 237). Purification was accomplished most generally "by way of the sacraments" (p. 235; see also Louth, 1986). Among the sacraments, baptism symbolized purification most precisely. "By dying to sin in baptism one could say mystically that he shares in the death of Christ himself" (Pseudo-Dionysius, 1987, p. 207). "The singing and reading of the scriptures" were directly efficacious. Reading scripture was a means of hierarchical ascension:

Minds turned off inferior things and disposed to holiness will draw from these [readings] the holy power of protection against all relapse into evil. They fully purify anyone needing something to be completely holy. They lead the sacred people to the divine images with which they can enter into their vision and communion. They nourish the perfect, filling them and unifying their likeness to the One with blessed and conceptual sights. (pp. 227–28)

Purification led to illumination because sacramental rites were symbols of conceptual realities. "The hierarchic rites are the precise images of these realities" (p. 207). "Sacred symbols are actually the perceptible tokens of the conceptual things. They show the way to them and lead to them, and the conceptual things are the source and the understanding underlying the perceptible manifestations of hierarchy" (p. 205). Purification was accomplished when perceptible phenomena ceased to be appreciated in a secular fashion and were instead experienced as symbolic representations of the holy and divine.

Illumination was apparently accomplished through visual imagination. Infinite light was a synonym for illumination (p. 165), and pseudo-Dionysius provided explicit instructions concerning the practice of visualization as a means to cultivate angelic visions:

Let us, then, call upon Jesus, the Light of the Father, the "true light enlightening every man coming into the world," "through whom we have obtained access" to the Father, the light which is the source of all light. To the best of our abilities . . . we should behold the intelligent hierarchies of heaven. . . . We must lift up the immaterial and steady eyes of our minds to that outpouring of Light which is so primal, indeed much more so, and which comes from that source of divinity, I mean the Father. This is the Light which, by way of representative symbols, makes known to us the most blessed hierarchies among the angels. But we need to rise from this outpouring of illumination so as to come to the simple ray of Light itself. (pp. 145–46).

Possibly alluding to the crucified angels in the Syriac mystery of the cross, pseudo-Dionysius recommended beholding, which is to say, visualizing the angels in imaginary forms. Angels themselves are incorporeal and intelligible; their representation in mental images was intrinsically metaphoric or allegorical.

The experience of Jesus as "the simple ray of Light itself" was similarly to be understood not literally but metaphorically, whether as a literary trope or as a mental image appropriate for visualization. For precise theological purposes, pseudo-Dionysius (1987) referred to Jesus explicitly as "transcendent mind, utterly divine mind."

Let your respect for the things of the hidden God be shown in knowledge that comes from the intellect and is unseen. . . . Indeed the

Word of God teaches those of us who are its disciples that in this fashion—though more clearly and more intellectually—Jesus enlightens our blessed superiors, Jesus who is transcendent mind, utterly divine mind, who is the source and the being underlying all hierarchy, all sanctification, all the workings of God, who is the ultimate in divine power. He assimilates them, as much as they are able, to his own light. As for us, with that yearning for beauty which raises us upward (and which is raised up) to him, he pulls together all our many differences. (pp. 195–96)

The intellect was described metaphorically as divine light. Properly understood, it was "transcendent mind, utterly divine mind," a rank of being higher than any mental image.

One experience was still higher. "The unknowing of what is beyond being is something above and beyond speech, mind, or being itself" (p. 49). A self-report by pseudo-Dionysius tends to suggest, however, that apprehension of the fact of God's transcendence was attained during an experience that started differently:

The vision revealed to the theologian came from one of those holy and blessed angels assigned to look after us. Under the illuminating guidance of the angel he was raised up to such a sacred contemplation that, if I may speak in symbols, he was able to look upon the most superior beings established under, around, and with God. He was able to look beyond those beings to that summit, beyond every source, enthroned amid the subordinate powers, and yet super-ineffably transcending them and all things. In this vision the theologian learned that the Deity surpasses every visible and invisible power in a total excess of transcendence. It is completely set apart from everything. It is unlike even the foremost of beings. It is the Cause and the source of being for every entity. (p. 179)

Pseudo-Dionysius referred to his ecstatic itinerary in Neoplatonic terms as a reversion (*epistrophe*) and uplifting (*anagoge*) (McGinn, 1991, p. 171). He summarized it as follows:

It is not for nothing that the blessed Moses is commanded to submit first to purification and then to depart from those who have not undergone this. When every purification is complete, he hears the many-voiced trumpets. He sees the many lights, pure and with rays streaming abundantly. Then, standing apart from the crowds and accompanied by chosen priests, he pushes ahead to the summit of the divine ascents. And yet he does not meet God himself, but contemplates, not him who is invisible, but rather where he dwells. This means, I presume, that the holiest and highest of the things perceived with the eye of the body or the mind are but the rationale which presupposes all that lies below the Transcendent One. Through them, however, his unimaginable presence is shown. (pseudo-Dionysius, 1987, pp. 136–37)

Interpreters have traditionally emphasized pseudo-Dionysius' advice to reject lower levels once upper ones had been attained. "As we climb from the last things up to the most primary we deny all things so that we may unhiddenly know that unknowing which itself is hidden from all those possessed of knowing amid all beings" (p. 138). In the present context, I would instead emphasize that the lower levels were pseudo-Dionysius' means to attain the higher ones. The relationship was not anagogical, with lower levels mirroring higher ones (Barnett, 2000, pp. 123–24). Purification, once completed, inspired auditory and visual experiences that together comprised illumination. Purification and illumination respectively concerned "the things perceived with the eye of the body or the mind." When perceptible and imaginable phenomena were appreciated as symbols, their very coherence constituted an experience of intellect or rationale, which was the Logos. In its turn, the Logos implied the unimaginable presence of the Transcendent One.

Pseudo-Dionysius affirmed the distinction made by Origen and Evagrius Ponticus regarding *praktike* and two kinds of contemplation (McGinn, 1991, p. 172). The two contemplations concerned the immanence and transcendence of God, respectively. These corresponded approximately to the distinction in Neoplatonism between union with the *nous* and union with the One or Ineffable (Merlan, 1963). Origen's triad should not be equated, however, with pseudo-Dionysius' triad of purification, illumination, and perfection. Plotinus had maintained a triad of life (Soul), mind (Intellect), and being (the One); and the Cappadocian Fathers, St. Basil of Caesarea and St. Gregory of Nyssa (c. 335–c. 395), had followed Plotinus when they maintained that matter is an illusion generated by Soul and Intellect (Armstrong, 1955, p. 55). Iamblichus and the later Neoplatonists distinguished the Ineffable from the One and counted physical matter as a genuine level of reality. Mystical reversions proceeded no higher than the One, however, because both reduction to the One and the unknowing of the Ineffable were accomplished at the level of Intellect. Pseudo-Dionysius' triad of purification, illumination, and perfection parallelled later Neoplatonism, as an ascension through material sacraments, imagistic visions, and conceptual thoughts, respectively. There was no higher level of ascension because both types of contemplation occurred at the intellectual level. The immanence of God was not transcended when his transcendence was contemplated. "Union with him who is beyond all being and knowledge" remained "a sight of the mysterious things" (pseudo-Dionysius, 1987, p. 135; McGinn, 1991, p. 179).

Pseudo-Dionysius' program of sacraments, imagistic visions, and intellectual apprehensions of the fact of God's transcendence, constituted his mystical itinerary. He permitted sense perceptions to inspire symbolic images, and images to generate concepts that allowed him to move beyond imagery into the purely conceptual. Much as the itinerary suited meditations on the passion, pseudo-Dionysius' theology was too voluntaristic and theurgical for Western Christian tastes.

Early in the medieval appropriation of pseudo-Dionysius, Hugh of St. Victor wrote a *Commentary on the Celestial Hierarchy* that popularized pseudo-Dionysius' views on hierarchy and symbolism (McGinn, 1976, p. 212). Hugh built on pseudo-Dionysius' three stage itinerary in proposing his own quadripartite model. Hugh's itinerary was not an ecstatic one, however. The first stage, awakening, entailed fear, sorrow and love; purgation involved patience, mercy, and compunction. The third stage, illumination, included thinking and meditation together with contemplation; and the final stage of union pertained to action in the world, by means of temperance, prudence, and fortitude (McGinn, 1994, p. 382). Hugh's magisterial deployment of mental images, for example, in *Noah's Ark* (Hugh, 1962), remained within the Western monastic tradition of recollection or nonmystical meditation; while his views on contemplation pertained to intellectual visions alone. There was no progression, as there was in pseudo-Dionysius, from one type of ecstasy to another. Hugh went only as far as Augustine had done in asserting that sense perceptions inevitably generate memories, which are a type of imagination; and that imaginations are a necessary foundation for conceptual thoughts, including the contemplation of God. Hugh stated: "It is impossible to represent invisible things except by means of those which are visible. Therefore all theology of necessity has recourse to visible representations in order to make known the invisible" (as cited in Zinn, 1973, p. 319). A generation later, Richard of St. Victor (d. 1173) similarly maintained that "reason never rises up to cognition of the invisible unless her handmaid, imagination, represents to her the form of visible things" (Richard, 1979, p. 57). These efforts to psychologize imagination did not go unchallenged. Albertus Magnus and St. Thomas Aquinas both affirmed the traditional view that demons cause illusions and false visions (Erickson, 1976, p. 38).

THE THEOLOGICAL STATUS OF MYSTICAL DEATH

When twelfth century churchmen began to experience mystical deaths through meditation on the passion, they found themselves confronted by a spiritual phenomenon that had not been addressed by Latin authorities of the patristic era: Cassian, Benedict, Augustine, and Gregory. The capacity of meditation on the passion to induce experiences of mystical death posed a theological problem. There was no *ligatura*. Was crucifixion with Christ to be considered a vision? If so, its cultivation through meditation made it theurgical and illicit. If it was instead licit, it had to be nothing more than a meditation. What then was one to think of the final phase of the experience, when images of being crucified were replaced by contemplations of God?

Medieval writers did not pose these potentially heretical questions as bluntly as I have done, but they provided responses to them. The question of the practice's legitimacy was the easiest to answer. Mystical death was a venerable meditation of the Syriac Church, and St. Paul bore witness to its theological validity. Paul wrote: "I have been crucified with Christ; it is no longer I who live, but Christ who lives in me" (Galatians 2:20). "We know that our old self was crucified with him so that the sinful body might be destroyed, and we might no longer be enslaved to sin. For he who has died is freed from sin. But if we have died with Christ, we believe that we shall also live with him" (Romans 6:6–8). "For as in Adam all die, so also in Christ shall all be made alive. . . . Just as we have borne the image of the man of dust, we shall also bear the image of the man of heaven" (1 Corinthians 15:22, 49).

Granting its legitimacy, was mystical death nothing more than a meditation? If so, what was one to make of the contemplative state that was its sequel? What was the relation between mystical death and resurrection? How was it possible for meditation to induce contemplation, without the latter being theurgical, demonic, and illicit? To answer these questions, Bernard, Bonaventure, and Hilton developed a mystical theology whose psychological sophistication was unprecedented in Christian history.

Bernard's system of mystical theology addressed these questions, among other manners, by ignoring Gregory's simplistic formulations and instead reverting to the learned tradition of Augustine. Bernard affirmed both the possibility and the validity of seeking the category of visions that Augustine had called "spiritual" and that medieval writers were to call imaginative and interior:

> It is . . . within the power of each of us, even during the time of our mortal life, to hollow out a place anywhere we will in the heavenly wall: at our pleasure to visit the patriarchs now, to salute the prophets now, to mingle with the assembly of apostles now, to slip into the choirs of martyrs now, even to run with all the swiftness of mind that devotion can inspire through the orders and dwellings of the blessed spirits, from the smallest angel to the Cherubim and Seraphim. And if we stand and knock there where our attraction has drawn us, inwardly moved as the Spirit wills, [the door] will at once be opened

to us, a cranny will be made amid the holy mountains—or rather the holy minds—who will spontaneously and lovingly enfold us that we may rest with them for a while. The face and voice of every soul who acts like this are pleasing to God: the face for its candor, the voice for its praise. For praise and beauty are in his sight. (Bernard, 1979, pp. 151–52)

Bernard was describing the contents of imaginative visions when he claimed that God is pleased by the beauty of the mystic's face while the mystic sings divine praises in heaven. Bernard did not specify how a person was to stand and knock in order to join the heavenly company. He affirmed, however, that imaginative visions could be sought, and that holy minds would respond favorably to visionaries who sought to visit with them in heaven. The phrase "holy minds" indicated that Bernard believed that heavenly angels and saints were themselves purely intellectual beings. Imaginative visions portrayed them as though they had envisionable forms, but the forms were to be understood as sense-derived symbols that represented holy intelligences.

Bernard attributed the imaginative contents of imaginative visions to the work of angels. He wrote:

I cannot see what this [Song of Songs 1:11] may mean if not the construction of certain spiritual images in order to bring the purest intuitions of divine wisdom before the eyes of the soul that contemplates, to enable it to perceive, as though puzzling reflections in a mirror, what it cannot possibly gaze on as yet face to face. . . . when the spirit is ravished out of itself and granted a vision of God that suddenly shines into the mind with the swiftness of a lightning-flash, immediately, but whence I know not, images of earthly things fill the imagination, either as an aid to understanding or to temper the intensity of the divine light. So well-adapted are they to the divinely illumined senses, that in their shadow the utterly pure and brilliant radiance of the truth is rendered more bearable to the mind and more capable of being communicated to others. My opinion is that they are formed in our imaginations by the inspirations of the holy angels, just as on the other hand there is no doubt that evil suggestions of an opposite nature are forced upon us by the bad angels. (Bernard, 1976, pp. 206–7)

Bernard here explained that spiritual images are intuitions of divine wisdom that are perceived by the imagination or eyes of the soul as images of earthly things. The term "contemplation" was appropriately used in reference to imaginative visions, but the phenomena were of a secondary order. Spiritual images were not divine, but were "formed in our imaginations by the inspirations of the holy angels."

Bernard also adhered to Augustine's view of the doctrinal significance of intellectual visions. In Augustine's view, original sin had two continuing consequences: sexual desire and ignorance. These failings caused humanity to differ from the image of God in which it was made. Of all that humanity has been since the fall of Adam, it is not the whole person, nor even the whole soul, but only the mind that has the distinction of being an image of God. The image of God that is the human mind can be deformed through sin, but it cannot be lost. It is always capable of being reformed through grace. Reformation requires the mind's emergence from the sensible images that cover it, so that the mind may be experienced in its own true nature as intrinsically and purely intellectual. The mind achieves this reformation through the contemplation of God. In mirroring the pure intellectuality of God, the mind is occupied in pure intellectuality and so regains its intrinsic and pure nature (Gilson, 1960, pp. 151, 213–14, 219, 221, 223).

In keeping with these teachings of Augustine, Bernard maintained that intellectual visions were the means through which the soul recovered the image of God that had been corrupted at Adam's fall (Bernard, 1976, p. 179; 1980, p. 34). Among the varieties of intellectual vision that a contemplative might know, it was above all spiritual marriage with the Word that conformed the soul to the image of God. Bernard wrote:

> There is a place where God is seen in tranquil rest, where he is neither Judge nor Teacher but Bridegroom. . . . appearing before him in his holy place, they [souls] . . . become sharers in the inheritance of the Son to whose image they were to be conformed. (Bernard, 1976, p. 38)

Spiritual marriage was to be prized not as an end in itself, but because it had the function of conforming the soul to the image of God, in whose image it was made. Spiritual marriage prepared the soul by making it eligible for the afterlife in heaven.

Mystical death had no comparable role to play. Its virtue consisted in purging the soul of sin, by way of preparation for the transformative experience of an intellectual contemplation. Summarizing mystical death and spiritual marriage, Bernard offered an image that was based on communion: "I am chewed as I am reproved by him; I am swallowed as I am taught; I am digested as I am changed; I am assimilated as I am transformed; I am made one as I am conformed" (Bernard, 1980, p. 52). Explaining the sequence in simpler language, Bernard also wrote:

Let me die the death of angels that, transcending the memory of things present, I may cast off not only the desire for what are corporeal and inferior but even their images, that I may enjoy pure conversation with those who bear the likeness of purity.

This kind of ecstasy, in my opinion, is alone or principally called contemplation. Not to be gripped during life by material desires is a mark of human virtue; but to gaze without the use of bodily likenesses is the sign of angelic purity. . . . You have advanced, you have placed yourself apart, but you have not yet put yourself at a distance, unless you succeed in flying with purity of mind beyond the material images that press in from every side. Until that point promise yourself no rest. (Bernard, 1979, p. 53)

In Bernard's view, the soul's restoration could not be achieved through an imaginative vision, because the image of God was not a corporeal image. It was necessary to cast off images of the corporeal and material in order to attain the purity of mind or intellect that is necessary for contemplation. Importantly, Bernard used the term "ecstasy" in reference to casting off material images. He evidently believed that the grace that chastized during a mystical death might be revealed as a contemplative state through the abandonment of mental images, even though the images that were being abandoned had been cultivated through meditation.

Bernard's concept of a shift from meditation to contemplation, involving the soul's cooperation with divine grace, represented a novelty in Latin mystical theology. It was conventional to regard meditation as a request that was graciously answered with a contemplation. In conceptualizing mystical death and resurrection, Bernard addressed the circumstance when grace responded before the act of meditating had been completed. He suggested that people who found their meditations being facilitated by grace might immediately suspend further mental imaging and instead contemplate the grace intellectually. Bernard did not develop the idea further; but Bonaventure's formulation can be seen as its corollary.

BONAVENTURE'S INNOVATION

Bernard advocated conformance with the lifestyle that the gospels attributed to Jesus: "What does it mean to eat his flesh and drink his blood, if not to share in his sufferings and to imitate the way of life he led in the flesh?" (Bernard, 1981, p. 132). However, the Cistercian reformation that Bernard championed interpreted imitation of Jesus' way of life to refer to the cloister. The Cistercians had reformed monastic life by reverting to a simple and strict interpretation of the Rule of St. Benedict. Francis of Assisi treated the imitation of Christ more literally. He rejected monastic life as an unacceptable compromise with Jesus' way of life. Francis sought a homeless, impoverished, wandering ministry of preaching and helping in conformity with the gospel narratives of the life of Jesus. His Christology was integral to his purpose of ministry to the laity. He sought to bring conformance with Christ to the general public.

Francis's embrace of the itinerant lifestyle that the gospels attributed to Jesus gave new meaning to the traditional doctrine of conformance with the image of God. Possibly it was Francis's ambition; certainly it was his effect. *The Little Flowers of St. Francis*, an enormously popular vernacular (Tuscan) text of the fourteenth century (Fleming, 1977, p. 60), begins with the statement, "First, it is to be considered that the glorious St. Francis in all the acts of his life was conformed to Christ the blessed" (Ugolino, 1958, p. 3). This popular view of Francis arose within a very short time of his death. Bonaventure interpreted the stigmata, poverty, and humility of Francis of Assisi as evidence that conformance with God pertained not only to the mind, but also to the body and lifestyle (Delio, 1998, pp. 81, 91). By the end of the thirteenth century, in Jacopone da Todi's hymns, Francis was characterized almost as a re-incarnation of Christ. Underhill remarked that no other saint has ever been described in similar terms. "No one but St. Francis left behind him the reputation of a success so genuine, that it could be said and sung of him in all sincerity 'It seemed as if Christ had come again; that very Christ who died upon the Rood'" (Underhill, 1933, pp. 164–65). Francis's achievement made the soul's transformation credible, vivid, and widely understood as a realistic possibility for human behavior in the world.

Franciscan spirituality was to develop the notion further. Bonaventure never deviated from the letter of Augustinian theology. He asserted, for example, "the reality of the image [of God] is found only in intellectual creatures or rational spirits; the reality of the similitude is found only in those who are conformed to God" (as cited in Hayes, 1999, p. 90). Again, "lying totally in these things of sense, it [the soul] cannot reenter into itself as into the image of God" (Bonaventure, 1978, p. 87). Nevertheless, by relying on the idea of "levels, as it were on the rungs of a ladder" (as cited in Hayes, 1999, p. 90), Bonaventure created a place within Augustine's pure intellectualism for Francis's human innovation.

At the very end of *The Mystical Vine*, Bonaventure discussed conformance with the image of the passion as a preludge to the soul's reformation through its intellectual divinization. "O most sweet and good Jesus, *Father of Lights* . . . grant that . . . we may be so completely and fully restored to Your favor that, conforming to the image of Your passion, we may also be reformed to the image of Your divinity" (Bonaventure, 1960, pp. 204–5). Bonaventure here added a novel detail to Bernard's doctrine. Where Bernard had contrasted the death of angels with spiritual marriage, because the one was an imaginative vision and only an intellectual vision might be transformative, Bonaventure regarded mystical death as a prelude to the soul's transformation through spiritual resurrection. Mystical death was itself a conformity to the image of Jesus. It was not, however, a restoration of the intellectual image of God.

Bonaventure's best known work, *The Mind's Journey into God*, discusses contemplation, which Bonaventure divided by topic into seven chapters. The chapter titles are:

1. On the stages of the ascent into God and on contemplation through His vestiges in the universe.
2. On contemplating God in His vestiges in the sense world.
3. On contemplating God through His image stamped upon our natural powers.
4. On contemplating God in His image reformed by the gifts of grace.
5. On contemplating the divine unity through its primary name which is Being.
6. On contemplating the most blessed Trinity in its name which is Good.
7. On spiritual and mystical ecstasy in which rest is given to our intellect when through ecstasy our affection passes over entirely into God. (Bonaventure, 1978, pp. 59, 69, 79, 87, 94, 102, 110)

Only the second and seventh topics had been considered contemplation in the monastic tradition that contemplated the world of nature and God in his essence. Inclusion of the other topics imparted an original sense to the word "contemplation." The term had traditionally referred to the soul's response to an intellectual vision that it had been granted by divine grace. The soul contemplated what grace disclosed. Bonaventure extended the term to include acts of thinking intellectually on a variety of theological topics. In this way, Bonaventure blurred the distinction between thinking voluntarily about God's manifestation in the world, and between being shown God's manifestation in the world in an intellectual vision. In both cases, it was God's true manifestation that was being thought about; in both cases the thinking was accurate; in both cases the thinking was possible only through grace. What then did it matter whether the contemplative was in an alternate state of consciousness?

Because "knowing the truth is an exercise or actualization of intellectual light" that proceeds through grace (Aquinas, *Summa Theologiae*, 1a2ae. 109, 1), successful meditation was attributed to cooperative grace "in which our mind is both a mover and is moved, [and] the operation is attributed not only to God but also to the soul" (111, 2). Medieval theology did not dwell systematically on the soul's contribution to cooperative grace. Aquinas wrote only in passing of "a gratuitous capacity supplementing the capacity of his [man's] nature . . .

to perform and will the supernatural good" (109, 2). In cases when the grace was habitual, and did not "cease to exist as soon as the act stops," it was possible also to speak in passing of "gratuitous habits" of the soul (Aquinas, *Summa Contra Gentiles*, III, ii, Ch 154, 25; Ch 155, 10). Aquinas recognized that "grace . . . is an accidental form of the soul itself" (*Summa Theologiae*, 1a2ae. 110, 2); but he failed to address the corollary that a form, once created in a soul by operative grace, may become a permanent part of the soul that the soul is able to deploy voluntarily—as, for example, knowledge of God's existence and love, and so forth.

Bonaventure drew the logical conclusion. He extended use of the term "contemplation" to include what had previously been contrasted as meditation. He ceased to contrast meditation and contemplation as natural and supernatural, respectively. Contemplation was an instance of cooperative grace, and to the extent that meditations were facilitated by grace, they too were instances of cooperative grace.

Bonaventure briefly discussed meditation on the passion in a complementary fashion at the very end of *The Mind's Journey*:

> Only he truly perceives who says: *My soul chooses hanging and my bones death*. Whoever loves this death can see God because it is true beyond doubt that *man will not see me and live*. Let us, then, die and enter into the darkness; let us impose silence upon our cares, our desires and our imaginings. With Christ crucified let us pass *out of this world to the Father*. (Bonaventure, 1978, pp 15–16)

Meditation on the passion that culminated in mystical death permitted a person to see God, that is, to contemplate theological topics. Like all meditations, the contemplations might be facilitated by grace, but they were not visions in Augustine's sense of the term. They were instances of cooperative grace. Contemplation of God's existence and all other topics of affirmative knowledge about God necessarily superadded divine grace to the soul's natural capacity for knowledge.

Contemplation was not to be confused with the ecstasy of passing over into God (de Vinck, 1960, p. 62). The soul's natural powers were not merely superadded to, but entirely eclipsed and uninvolved in the mind's passage beyond contemplation into the darkness of the Father. Rahner (1979) noted that Bonaventure consistently used the term ecstasy in reference to the teaching of pseudo-Dionysius. In Bonaventure's usage, passing over into God was not a contemplative knowledge of God that was mediated by grace. Bonaventure discussed ecstasy in terms of *sentire* rather than *cognoscere*, experiencing rather than knowing, in apparent emphasis of the emotional dimension of ecstatic love that was integral to the moment of union (pp. 117–20). Passing over into God, which Aquinas termed "the vision of God in His essence" (*Summa Contra Gentiles* III ii, Ch 151, 3), was an experience of unknowing.

What pseudo-Dionysius and Bonaventure described was a contemplation not of nothing, but of negative theological formulations that culminated in an experience of ecstasy. Bonaventure (1960) wrote:

> We must raise it [the heart] aloft, above anything perceptible, imaginable, or conceivable, in this way: first, looking straight upon Him whom we desire to love perfectly, we realize that this Beloved cannot be perceived through the senses, since He is neither seen, nor heard, smelled, tasted, or touched: thus, He is not perceptible; yet *He is all delight*. Next, we realize that He cannot be seen through the imagination, since He has no shape, figure, quantity, limitation, or mutability: thus, He is unimaginable; yet *He is all delight*. Finally, we realize that He cannot be conceived through the intellect, since He is beyond demonstration, definition, opinion, estimation, or investigation: thus, He is inconceivable: yet *He is all delight*. (p. 71)

Bonaventure apparently included the ecstasy of the pseudo-Dionysian *via negationis* within the scope of his understanding of meditation.

Bonaventure's account of ecstasy has often been interpreted out of its historical context as a reference to a mystical experience of divine nothingness, such as was advocated by Meister Eckhart (Forman, 1990), or in *The Cloud of Unknowing* (Wolters, 1961). Mystics then report experiences that seemingly have no content. There is consciousness, but consciousness has no apparent objects. These experiences are, in my view, instances of dissociation, of the *ligatura*, that are so complete that nothing else can be experienced. In all events, Bonaventure clearly discussed God as unknowable; nowhere did he claim that God was knowably nothingness.

For Bonaventure, contemplation of God was a contemplation of theology and, as such, a sort of meditation on intellectual topics. Because the question of a vision in Augustine's sense of the term arose only in connection with the pseudo-Dionysian ecstasy of unknowing, the meditative experiences were intrinsically licit. Bonaventure's theological move, which became conventional for Franciscan spirituality, was later adopted by Ignatius of Loyola (1991) in his definition of spiritual exercises as "every method of examination of conscience, meditation, contemplation, vocal or mental prayer, and other spiritual activities" (p. 121).

Not only did Bonaventure extend use of the term "contemplation" in *The Mind's Journey*, but he referred equally broadly to meditation in *De Triplici Via alias Incendium Amoris*, "*The Triple Way or Love Enkindled*," where he revived pseudo-Dionysius's tripartite division of the mystic path into the purgative, illuminative, and perfective ways. For present purposes, it is significant that Bonaventure referred to meditation in the course of his discussions of *each of the three stages*. Meditation on the passion was first performed during purgation:

> Man should fix his gaze upon three things: the HOUR OF DEATH, so imminently close; the BLOOD OF THE CROSS, so recently shed; the FACE OF THE JUDGE, so verily present. This three fold thought will sharpen the sting of conscience against all evil. (Bonaventure, 1960, p. 66)

Where Bernard had contrasted the death of angels with spiritual marriage as separate experiences, the one meditative and the other contemplative, Bonaventure apparently regarded mystical death and resurrection as a unified process of "purgation by way of meditation. . . . This first way originates in the sting of conscience, and terminates in a disposition of spiritual joy; it is pursued in pain, but consummated in love" (p. 70).

Bonaventure also treated meditation as the operative principle of the illuminative way. In "the illuminative way . . . the light of intelligence must be turned back through meditation. Man must return to the Fountainhead of all good by remembering the promised rewards" (p. 70). Among other instructions for the meditative construction of appropriate remembrances, Bonaventure counselled: "Consider why He is suffering, and forget yourself in a rapture of devotion" and "Consider what follows upon His suffering, and behold the light of truth through the eyes of contemplation" (pp. 82, 84). Having gone through mystical death, one was to reflect on the theological implications of the experience.

Lastly, Bonaventure employed the term "meditation" in reference to the perfective way (p. 72). Bonaventure explained that the perfective way ends in negative theology, in the ecstatic experience of knowing the fact of God's radical transcendence, his utter unknowability.

> As Denis says: "(When applied to God,) affirmations are inadequate, while negations are wholly true." Negations seem to say less but actually they say more. This manner of elevation consists in using nothing but negative predications, and that in a way which is orderly, proceeding from the lowest to the highest, but which also expresses transcendence. For instance, we say: God is not perceptible through the senses, but is above the senses; nor is He imaginable, intelligible, manifest, but is above all these concepts. Then the vision of truth, having experienced the night of the intellect, rises higher and penetrates deeper, because it exceeds the intellect itself as well as every created thing. This is the most noble manner of elevation. (p. 93)

In associating mystical death with purgation and illumination, and the resurrection or pseudo-Dionysian ecstasy with the final perfection, Bonaventure indicated that mystical death and resurrection contains the whole of the triple way within it. He wrote: "The cross itself is the key, the door, the way, and the splendor of truth" (Bonaventure, 1960, p. 86). Meditation on the passion is purgative in its precipitation of a mystical death. It becomes illuminative through the resurrection, which consists at minimum of the realization that one is still alive, well, and having an experience of grace. Finally, meditation on the passion becomes perfective when reflection on the fact of contemplation leads to apprehension of the fact of God's transcendence.

For Western Christianity, Bonaventure's formulation represented an enormous advance in psychological sophistication. Augustine had given his approval to the comparatively simplistic seeing-is-believing approach to religious experiences that the Desert Fathers had developed. Working implicitly with the concept of cooperative grace, Bonaventure suggested that what seemed to be passive experiences of the soul were not always so. The soul's agency was greater than had been appreciated. It extended to most of what had traditionally been called contemplation. Grace was at work in it, but so too was human nature.

WALTER HILTON'S SOLUTION

The gap between the formulations of Bernard and Bonaventure was managed by Walter Hilton, whose adept handling of scholastic theology attests to his training as a theologian. Owen (1971) remarked that as innovative as Hilton was, "there is not the slightest hint of any gap between experience and interpretation, contemplation and dogma" (p. 37). Hilton acknowledged that imaginations are inferior to intellections, but he justified meditation on the passion with the pragmatic claim that novices invariably begin with corporeal imaginations and only proceed to intellections as they progress in spirituality.

> It is very hard for a soul that is rough and much in the flesh to have sight and knowledge of itself, or of an angel or of God; it falls at once into the imagination of a bodily shape, and it supposes by that to have the sight of itself, and so of God, and so of spiritual things; and that cannot be. For all spiritual things are seen and known by the understanding of the soul, not by imagination. Just as a soul sees by understanding that the virtue of justice is to yield to each thing what it ought to have, so likewise the soul can see itself by understanding.
>
> Nevertheless, I do not say that your soul is to rest still in this knowledge, but by this it shall seek higher knowledge above itself, and

that is the nature of God. For your soul is only a mirror in which you shall see God spiritually. Therefore, you shall first find your mirror and keep it bright and clean from fleshly filth and worldly vanity, and hold it well up from the earth so that you can see it, and in it likewise our Lord. (p. 253)

Unlike other meditations, meditation on the passion has the power to cultivate an imaginative meditation that, through grace, may lead directly to an intellectual contemplation. Although the the intellectual contemplation alone restores the image of God, the integral connection between mystical death and its intellectual sequel validated Bonaventure's position that the restoration of the image of Jesus in his humanity was to be achieved first.

Where Bernard and William of St. Thierry had regarded mystical death as the reaction of a guilty conscience to actual grace, Hilton asserted that the development of meditation on the passion into a mystical death was due to "an opening of the eye of the spirit." It was a meditation that was enhanced "by the grace of the Holy Spirit":

When the remembrance of Christ's passion or any point of his humanity is thus caused in your heart by such spiritual vision, with devout affection answering to it—then, know well that it is not your own doing, neither the pretense of any wicked spirit, but by the grace of the Holy Spirit. For it is an opening of the eye of the spirit into Christ's humanity. (p. 106)

For Hilton as for Bonaventure, meditation on the passion was an act of imagination that was within the scope of human nature. The development of the mental imagery into a mystical death was facilitated by grace and was a necessary prelude to contemplation. Agreeing with Bernard, Hilton added that mystical death is "a great help in destroying great sins" (p. 106).

In another passage, Hilton phrased the same teaching about meditation on the passion destroying sins in specifically Augustinian terms of the destruction of the image of God that had been corrupted through original sin:

Then what are you to do with this image? I answer you with a word that the Jews said to Pilate about Christ: *Tolle, tolle, crucifige eum!* ["Take him away! Take him away! Crucify him!" John 19:15] Take this body of sin and put it upon the cross. That is to say, Break down this image and slay the false love of sin in yourself. As Christ's body was slain for our trespasses, so, if you want to be like Christ you should slay your carnal appetite and the fleshly lust in yourself. So said St. Paul: *Qui autem Christi sunt, carnem suam crucifixerunt cum vitiis et concupiscentiis.* Those who are Christ's followers have crucified and slain their flesh (that is, the image of sin), with all the lusts and unreasoning appetites of it [Galatians 5:24]. (p. 156)

Hilton was not referring to the slaying of sins in a manner that was merely metaphoric. He used Augustinian language about the image of sin and its destruction in reference to meditation on the passion. In Augustine's usage, the image of sin, like the image of God, had referred to the soul's intellectual faculty. For Hilton, both images were corporeal imaginations. In writing of the image of sin, Hilton was offering a psychological theory of the latent meaning of a mystical death. The image of Christ's body that was seen in imagination signified the meditator's "flesh (that is, the image of sin)."

Hilton offered the same interpretation in the following passage, where he explained meditation on the image of Jesus as a meditation that actually concerned the image of the meditator's own soul:

Set your intention and purpose as if you wanted neither to seek, to feel nor to find anything but Jesus alone. This is troublesome, for vain thoughts are always wanting to press thickly into your heart, to draw your thought down to them; but you shall withstand them; and if you do, so you shall find something—though not Jesus whom you seek. What, then? Indeed, nothing but a dark and painful image of your own soul, which has neither the light of knowledge nor the feeling of love or pleasure. If you look at it plainly, this image is all wrapped up in black stinking clothes of sin, such as pride, envy, wrath, *accidie,* covetousness, gluttony, and lechery.

This is not the image of Jesus but it is an image of sin, as St. Paul calls it: a body of sin and a body of death. This image and this black shadow you carry about with you wherever you go. Many great streams of sin spring out of it, and small ones as well. Just as from the image of Jesus, if it were reformed in you, beams of spiritual light should rise up into heaven—such as burning desires, pure affections, wise thoughts, and virtues in all their honor—so from this image spring stirrings of pride, envy and others like them, which cast you down from the dignity of man into the likeness of a beast. (p. 124)

Hilton's concern with mental imagery led him to augment Augustine's reference to "an image of sin" by drawing on the language of Paul and speaking of the image of sin as "a body of sin and a body of death." Hilton's reference to death should not be thought casual. What appears during meditation on the passion to be Christ crucified is not the image of Jesus but an image of sin— an image of the meditator's own soul.

Hilton elsewhere summarized this original formulation with the notion that mystical death accomplishes the death of "the image of sin, of the old Adam." The "image of God" is purely spiritual and so awaits the resurrection:

> You are to put down the old man (that is, the image of sin and the old Adam) with all his members, for he is rotten with the desires of error, and you shall dress and clothe yourself in a new man, who is the image of God, through holiness, righteousness and the fullness of virtues. (p. 156)

Hilton's phrasing interpolated Augustine's concept of the image of sin within a paraphrase of Ephesians 4:22–24: "Put off your old nature which belongs to your former manner of life and is corrupt through deceitful lusts, and be renewed in the spirit of your minds, and put on the new nature, created after the likeness of God in true righteousness and holiness." Mystical death was not in any sense a vision of Jesus. Because mystical death was a meditation, the image that died was an image of the meditator's own soul, the old Adam, the image of sin.

Hilton's solution to the theological problem of mystical death was obvious in retrospect. His theory was implicit in the traditional understanding of meditation as recollection or remembering. Imaginations of events that had never been witnessed were understood to be constructed of images that were based on personal memories of sense perceptions. If the imaginative events included a mystical death, what died in imagination had necessarily to be the soul's own memories. No one prior to Hilton seems to have articulated this implication of the term "recollection," presumably because the seeing-is-believing patristic theology of visions had first to give way to the medieval view of cooperative grace. Only after Bonaventure ceased to underestimate the soul's contribution to contemplation was Hilton able to reconceptualize mystical death as the death not of Jesus, but of the old Adam.

CONCLUDING REFLECTIONS

The mystical theology of the monastic tradition had had no place within it for the practice of visualization. Mental images might be cultivated during meditations; but meditation was considered a natural activity of the soul. Meditation might be facilitated by divine grace; but it was not a gift of operative grace. It was an instance of cooperative grace that involved both the soul and God. Because meditation on the passion from the perspective of Jesus culminated in a mystical death that developed autonomously and was experienced passively, it posed a problem to the received tradition of monastic theology. A group of theological moves in the twelfth century may be appreciated as attempts to formulate an appropriate doctrine. The Victorine schoolmen, Hugh and Richard, pioneered the rehabilitation of imagination along pseudo-Dionysian lines. Bernard encouraged tolerance of the angelic production of angelic visions; and a series of visionaries, from Hildegard of Bingen through Joachim of Fiore and beyond, circulated original visions that they claimed to be revelatory and prophetic. Precedents for the visionaries were created through commentaries on the biblical book of Revelation that treated its images as allegorical visions of twelfth century events. However, the prophecies went unfulfilled and the rehabilitation of corporeal and imaginative visions proved simplistic.

In a passing remark, Aquinas seems to have opposed Bernard's theological move. Aquinas denied that visions that angels mediated were instances of grace:

> An angel purifies, illuminates and perfects angels or men by way of some sort of instruction, not by justifying them by grace. So Dionysius says that this kind of *purification, illumination and perfection is nothing other than the reception of divine knowledge.* (*Summa Theologiae*, 1a2ae. 112, 3)

Aquinas' treatment of purification, illumination, and perfection as stages of angelic instruction, but not of justification through grace, anticipated Bonaventure's equation of meditation and contemplation.

Sensing the dangers of encouraging superstitious veneration of private fantasies—many spiritual Franciscans endorsed the Joachite prophecies—Bonaventure followed Aquinas in opting not to enlarge the domain of claimed supernaturalism, but to reduce it. In *The Mind's Journey*, Bonaventure treated contemplations as though they were a variety of meditations. He acknowledged that grace facilitated the experiences, but he emphasized the soul's contributions as well. Bonaventure elsewhere associated meditation on the passion with each of the three stages of the *via mystica*, implicitly attributing mystical death to cooperative grace. Like Augustine's concept of memory, Bonaventure's equation of meditation with contemplation was an attempt to account for phenomena that we today would attribute to unconscious thinking.

Hilton's interpretation of the conversion of the image of sin into the image of Jesus proceeded within the scholastic tradition of Augustinian theology; but in identifying the image of Jesus as the human soul, Hilton followed Bonaventure in shifting the discussion from mystical theology to psychology. Hilton offered a psychological understanding of meditation on the passion, and his program of reforming in faith and feeling may justly be considered psychotherapeutic. Reforming in feeling was not a religious transformation that unwittingly anticipated the invention of psychotherapy. Hilton knowingly reformed human souls.

In crediting Hilton with the invention of psychotherapy, I am making the claim that he developed concepts of the human soul and its transformation that pertained to the same type of transformation as successful psychoanalysis does. I do not believe Hilton was able to achieve integrations of as much of the personality as psychoanalysts do today. Since Freud, psychoanalysis has repeatedly expanded both the variety of complaints that it is able to address successfully and the extent to which individual personalities become integrated. Hilton's achievement should be seen in a similar historical perspective. He developed his technique of spiritual direction for a very limited part of the medieval population, professional Christian religious, deeply convinced of their own sinfulness, who needed relief from reaction-formations that made them overly conscientious. Hilton's program aspired to the integration of aggression, but it left sexual inhibitions unaddressed. In claiming Hilton as Freud's forerunner, I am suggesting that in Hilton we meet the seed of what first became a sturdy sapling only in Freud's generation.

Afterword

Walter Hilton was the most popular spiritual writer of medieval England. The manuscripts of his texts are numerous, and they indicate interest in his thought by both Carthusians and Carmelites. Hilton is generally thought to have been the Middle English translator of the Latin *Stimulus amoris* of James of Milan. The translation, entitled *The Prickynge of Love*, survives in ten manuscripts. Hilton's name was attached to three manuscripts, including one at Cambridge (Hilton, 1952, p. 19). *The Prickynge of Love* was not published until 1952; but Hilton's major work on meditation on the passion, *The Scale of Perfection*, was written in Middle English and translated into Latin by Thomas Fyslake probably before 1400. The *Scale* was printed in its Middle English original by Wynkyn de Worde in 1494 at the request of Lady Margaret Beaufort, the mother of Henry VII (Hilton, 1991, p. 33). With the patronage of the King's Mother, the book sold well in early Tudor England, being republished by Julian Notary in 1507 and by de Worde in 1519, 1525, and 1533 (Gardner, 1936a).

Despite Hilton's local fame in late medieval and early Tudor England, he was forgotten by both the Protestant Reformation and the Catholic Counter-Reformation. Through Loyola and other spiritual directors of the Counter-Reformation, meditation on the passion from the perspective of an eye-witness achieved broad popularity, and meditation from the perspective of Jesus lapsed into obsolescence. As well, Hilton's ambition to produce structural character change through meditation was replaced by a trend to be satisfied with brief experiences of intense emotion. As a spiritual director, Hilton had aspired to a much more advanced level of spirituality—the sweetness of Jesus' temperament—than Catholics were generally interested in pursuing in the age of the Inquisition and the wars of religion.

Protestants neglected Hilton because he was a Catholic. However, the concept of personality integration that Hilton termed "reforming in faith and feeling" resurfaced among the English Puritans under the term "sanctification" (Mueller, 1991, p. 10). As Haartman (2004) demonstrated, the Puritans knew that the advanced spiritual state of sanctification occurred, but they had no knowledge of how to cultivate it. It was not until the eighteenth century that

John Wesley developed a technique for promoting sanctification. Wesley's procedure—the method for which Methodism became famous—bore no relation to meditation on the passion. Wesley combined "watching," a minute introspection and rejection of sinful desires, together with "praying," as he called the practice of the presence of God.

The enduring influence of Hilton may be seen in a further aspect of English culture from which his name was detached. Hilton's *Epistle on the Mixed Life* (in Hilton, 1929), a lesser work, survives in at least nineteen manuscripts of the fourteenth and fifteenth centuries; it was printed six times by 1517 (Beale, 1975, p. 382), which again attests to its popularity in the early Tudor period. Five surviving Tudor copies were bound together with the *Scale*. The *Epistle* counselled an English nobleman, who wished to practice contemplation, that he might do so without renouncing his aristocratic obligations. He could instead live a mixed life, partly of action in the world, and partly of contemplation. Prior to Hilton, the theological concept of a mixed life had been applied only to priests who had parish duties or administrative posts that made it impossible to live as contemplatives in monasteries. Hilton had the original idea that a lay person, no differently than a priest, could legitimately pursue contemplation on a part-time basis, while otherwise pursuing a life of action in the world. Hilton's proposal of a new social location for the practice of mysticism, outside the monastery in the secular community, articulated an idea that was formative for the emergence of Western esotericism. Beginning fifty years after Hilton's death, at the start of the Renaissance, it became commonplace for an aristocrat, a scholar, an artist, or another courtier also to be a part-time contemplative. By the late sixteenth century, the organization of mystical fraternities, whose members commonly engaged in mixed lives, was allegedly attempted by Giordano Bruno (Yates, 1964, p. 312 n. 5).

Although Hilton's program of spiritual direction was abandoned by Protestants and Catholics alike, the association of mystical death with human transformation reappeared in the Elizabethan period in connection with the mixed life of spiritual alchemists. Intriguingly, a copy of the Latin *Stimulus amoris* was owned by Dr. John Dee, court astrologer to Elizabeth I of England, and the author of *Monas Hieroglyphica* (1564), a foundation text of spiritual alchemy. Dee's copy is extant as Oxford, Corpus Christi College, MS 240 (Roberts & Watson, 1990, p. 181). In the early seventeenth century, the idea of a mystical fraternity that engaged in human transformation through mystical death was proposed in Rosicrucian literature that cited Dee's *Monas Hieroglyphica*; and a variant of the program was subsequently put into effect through the clandestine creation of Freemasonry.

Shakespeare bears witness that Hilton's legacy contributed to these Elizabethan developments of Western esotericism. The death and resurrection motifs that Shakespeare applied to Lear's episode of madness were integral to alchemical symbolism that runs throughout *King Lear* (Merkur, 2002, p. 280); and Shakespeare had Mercutio allude to *The Prickynge of Love* in *Romeo and Juliet*:

> *Romeo.* Is love a tender thing? It is too rough,
>   Too rude, too boisterous, and it pricks like thorn.
> *Mercutio.* If love be rough with you, be rough with love;
>   Prick love for pricking and you beat love down.
>   Give me a case to put my visage in:
>   A visor for a visor. What care I
>   What curious eye doth quote deformities?
>   Here are the beetle brows shall blush for me.
>   (I iv 24-32)

Mercutio's phrase "Prick love for pricking" played on the title of *The Prickynge of Love*. The allusion of Mercutio's name to that of Mercury indicated that the character was to be understood as a follower of the Hermetic Art, which is to say, alchemy. The character of Mercutio is sometimes thought to have been modelled specifically on the playwright Christopher Marlowe (Klein, 1961; Porter, 1988, pp. 135–44), who studied theology at Cambridge and may have been Shakespeare's source on Hilton. It is tempting to speculate that Shakespeare owed his extraordinary capacity for empathy to a degree of mental health that he had achieved, in part, through reforming in faith and feeling.

References

Adomnán of Iona. 1995. *Life of St. Columba*. Harmondsworth: Penguin Books.

Aelred of Rievaux. 1957. *A letter to his sister*. Trans. Geoffrey Webb and Adrian Walker. London: A. R. Mowbray & New York: Morehouse-Gorham.

———. 1971. *Treatises. The pastoral prayer*. Kalamazoo, MI: Cistercian Publications.

———. 2001. *The liturgical sermons: The first Clairvaux collection. Sermons one–twenty-eight. Advent– All Saints*. Trans. Theodore Berkeley and M. Basil Pennington. Kalamazoo, MI: Cistercian Publications.

Almond, Philip C. 1982. *Mystical experience and religious doctrine: An investigation of the study of mysticism in world religions*. Berlin & New York: Mouton Publishers.

Angela of Foligno. 1993. *Complete works*. Trans. Paul Lachance. New York: Paulist Press.

Anselm. 1973. *The prayers and meditations of Saint Anselm, with the Proslogion*. Trans. Benedicta Ward. Harmondsworth: Penguin Books.

Aquinas, Thomas. 1964. *Summa theologiae*. Latin text and English translation, introductions, notes, appendices and glossaries. Blackfriars, with London: Eyre & Spottiswoode, & New York: McGraw-Hill.

———. 1975. *Summa contra gentiles*. Trans. Vernon J. Bourke. Notre Dame & London: University of Notre Dame Press.

Arbman, Ernst. 1963–70. *Ecstasy or religious trance: In the experience of the ecstatics and from the scientific point of view*. 3 vols. Stockholm: Svenska Bokforlaget.

Armstrong, Arthur Hilary. 1955. Plotinus's doctrine of the infinite and its significance for Christian thought. *Downside Review* 73:47–58.

Augustine. 1982. *The literal meaning of Genesis*. Trans. John Hammond Taylor. New York & Ramsey, NJ: Newman Press.

———. 1998. *The city of God against the pagans*. Ed. and trans. R. W. Dyson. Cambridge: Cambridge University Press.

Bachelard, Gaston. 1987. *On poetic imagination and reverie: Selections from Gaston Bachelard*. Trans. Colette Gaudin. Dallas, TX: Spring Publications.

Baker, Denise N. 1999. The active and contemplative lives in Rolle, the *Cloud*-author and Hilton. In *The medieval mystical tradition England, Ireland and Wales*, ed. Marion

Glasscoe. 85–102. Exeter Symposium VI. Papers read at Charney Manor. Cambridge: D. S. Brewer.

Barnett, John. 2000. Mysticism and the liturgy in Denys the Areopagite. *Downside Review* 118:111–136.

Beale, Walter H. 1975. Walter Hilton and the concept of "medled lyf". *American Benedictine Review* 26 (4): 381–394.

Becker, Ernest. 1973. *The denial of death.* New York: Free Press.

Bell, David N. 1984. *The image and likeness: The Augustinian spirituality of William of St. Thierry.* Kalamazoo, MI: Cistercian Publications.

Bergler, Edmund. 1949. *The basic neurosis: Oral regression and psychic masochism.* New York: Grune & Stratton.

———. 1959. *Principles of self-damage.* New York: Philosophical Library. Rep. Madison, CT: International Universities Press, 1992.

Bernard of Clairvaux. 1971. *On the Song of Songs I.* Trans. Kilian Walsh. Cistercian Fathers Series 4. Kalamazoo, MI: Cistercian Publications, 1976.

———. 1976. *On the Song of Songs II.* Trans. Kilian Walsh. Cistercian Fathers Series 7. Kalamazoo, Mich.: Cistercian Publications.

———. 1979. *On the Song of Songs III.* Trans. Kilian Walsh & Irene M. Edmonds. Cistercian Fathers Series 31. Kalamazoo, MI: Cistercian Publications.

———. 1980. *On the Song of Songs IV.* Trans. Irene M. Edmonds. Cistercian Fathers Series 40. Kalamazoo, MI: Cistercian Publications.

———. 1981. *Sermons on conversion: On conversion, A sermon to clerics,* and *Lenten sermons on the Psalm 'He who dwells'.* Trans. Marie-Bernard Saïd. Kalamazoo, MI: Cistercian Publications.

———. 1995. Commentary to *On loving God,* by Emero Stiegman. Kalamazoo, MI: Cistercian Publications.

———. 2000. *The parables.* Trans. Michael Casey. *The sentences.* Trans. Francis R. Swietek. Ed. Maureen M. O'Brien. Kalamazoo, MI: Cistercian Publications.

Bestul, Thomas H. 1996. *Texts of the passion: Latin devotional literature and medieval society.* Philadelphia: University of Pennsylvania Press.

Bianchi, Enzo. 1998. *Praying the word: An introduction to* Lectio Divina. Trans. James W. Zona. Kalamazoo, MI: Cistercian Publications.

Bion, Wilfrid R. 1963. *Elements of psycho-analysis.* London: William Heinemann Medical Books. Repr. London: Karnac, 1984.

Birgitta of Sweden. 1990. *Life and selected revelations.* Trans. Albert Ryle Kezel. New York & Mahwah, NJ: Paulist Press.

Bishop, Donald H. 1994. Three medieval Christian mystics. In *Mysticism and the mystical experience: East and West,* ed. Donald H. Bishop., 62–109. Selinsgrove: Susquehanna University Press, & London and Toronto: Associated University Presses.

Blum, Richard, and Alexander Golitzin. 1991. *The sacred athlete: On the mystical experience and Dionysios, Its Westernworld Fountainhead.* Lanham, MD: University Press of America.

Blumenthal, Henry J. 1992. Soul vehicles in Simplicius. In *Platonism in late antiquity,* : eds. Stephen Gersh abd Charles, 173–88. Notre Dame, IN: University of Notre Dame Press.

Boenig, Robert (Intro.). 1990. *Contemplations of the dread and love of God (1506).* Delmar, NY: Scholars' Facsimiles & Reprints.

Bonaventure. 1907. *Stimulus Divini Amoris: That is, The Goad of divine love, very proper and profitable for all devout persons to read, written in Latin by the Seraphical Doctor S. Bonaventure, of the Seraphical Order of S. Francis.* Trans. B. Lewis A. Rev. and ed. W. A. Phillipson. London: R. and T. Washbourne, & New York: Benziger Bros.

———. 1960. *The works of Bonaventure: Cardinal, seraphic doctor and saint.* Vol. 1. *Mystical Opuscula,* trans. José de Vinck, 145–205. Paterson, NJ: St. Anthony Guild Press.

———. 1978. *The soul's journey into God. The Tree of Life. The life of St. Francis.* Trans. Ewart Cousins. New York: Paulist Press.

Bornkamm, Günther. 1971. *Paul.* Trans. D. M. G. Stalker. New York: Harper & Row.

Brenner, Ira. 2001. *Dissociation of trauma: Theory, phenomenology, and technique.* Madison, CT: International Universities Press.

Brierley, Marjorie. 1951. *Trends in psycho-analysis.* London: Hogarth Press & Institute of Psycho-Analysis.

Bruno, Giordano. 1964. *The heroic frenzies: A translation.* Trans. Paul Eugene Memmo, Jr. Chapel Hill: University of North Carolina Press.

Buber, Martin. 1917. *I and thou.* 2nd ed. Trans. Ronald Gregor Smith. Repr., New York: Charles Scribner's Sons, 1958.

Bynum, Caroline Walker. 1973. The spirituality of regular canons in the twelfth century: A new approach. *Medievalia et Humanistica* New Series 4:3–24.

Carruthers, Mary J. 1998. *The craft of thought: Meditation, rhetoric, and the making of images, 400–1200.* Cambridge: Cambridge University Press.

Casey, Michael. 1996a. *Sacred reading: The ancient art of Lectio Divina.* Liguori, MO: Liguori/Triumph.

———. 1996. *Toward God: The ancient wisdom of western prayer.* 2nd ed. Liguori, MO: Liguori/Triumph.

Caslant, Eugène. 1927. *Method of development of the supernormal faculties* [in French]. Meyer: Paris.

Cassian, John. 1997. *The conferences.* Trans. Boniface Ramsey. New York & Mahwah, NJ: Paulist Press.

Chadwick, Owen. 1968. *John Cassian.* 2nd ed. Cambridge: University Press.

Clark, James M. 1949. *The great German mystics: Eckhart, Tauler, and Suso.* Oxford: Basil Blackwell.

Clark, John P. H. 1977. The "lightsome darkness"—Aspects of Walter Hilton's theological background. *Downside Review* 95:95–109.

————. 1978a. The "Cloud of Unknowing," Walter Hilton and St. John of the Cross: A comparison. *Downside Review* 96:281–98.

————. 1978b. Walter Hilton and "liberty of spirit." *Downside Review* 96:61–78.

————. 1979. Action and contemplation in Walter Hilton. *Downside Review* 97:258–74.

————. 1984. Walter Hilton and the *Stimulus Amoris*. *Downside Review* 102:79–118.

Clark, John P. H., & Rosemary Dorward. 1991. Introduction. In *The scale of perfection,*. Walter Hilton, 33–68. New York & Mahwah, NJ: Paulist Press.

Cleve, Gunnel. 1994. *Mystic themes in Walter Hilton's* Scale of Perfection, Book 2. Salzburg Studies in English Literature, Elizabethan and Renaissance Studies 92:19:2. Salzburg, Austria: Institut für Anglistik und Amerikanistik, Universität Salburg, & Lewiston, NY: Edwin Mellen Press.

Coleman, T. W. 1935. Walter Hilton's "Scale of Perfection." *London Quarterly and Holborn Review* 160:241–45.

————. 1938. *English mystics of the fourteenth century*. London: Epworth Press. Repr. Westport, CT: Greenwood Press, 1971.

Corbin, Henry. 1954. *Avicenna and the visionary recital*. Trans. Willard R. Trask. Repr. Irving, TX: Spring, 1980.

————. 1971. *The man of light in Iranian Sufism*. Trans. Nancy Pearson. Repr. Boulder, CO: Shambhala, 1978.

Cousins, Ewert H. 1978. *Bonaventure and the coincidence of opposites*. Chicago: Franciscan Herald Press.

————. 1987. The humanity and the passion of Christ. In *Christian spirituality: High Middle Ages and Reformation*, ed. Jill Raitt, 375–91. New York: Crossroad.

Daniélou, Jean. 1973. *Gospel message and Hellenistic culture*. Trans. John Austin Baker. London: Darton, Longman & Todd, & Philadelphia: Westminster Press.

de Cisneros, Garcia Jimenez. 1929. *Book of exercises for the spiritual life: Written in the year 1500*. Trans. E. Allison Peers. Monastery of Montserrat.

de Gank, Roger, with John Baptist Hasbrouck trans. 1991. *The life of Beatrice of Nazareth, 1200–1268*. Kalamazoo, MI: Cistercian Publications.

de Nie, Giselle. 1987. *Views from a many-windowed tower: Studies of imagination in the works of Gregory of Tours*. Amsterdam: Rodopi.

de Verteuil, Michel. 1996. *Your word is a light for my steps*. Dublin: Veritas Publications.

de Vinck, José. 1960. Introductory note. In *The works of Bonaventure: Cardinal, seraphic doctor and saint*. Vol. 1. *Mystical Opuscula*, trans. José de Vinck, 61–62. Paterson, NJ: St. Anthony Guild Press.

Delacroix, Henri. 1908. *Études d'histoire et de psychologie du mysticism: Les grands mystiques Chrétiens.* Paris: Librairies Félix Alcan et Guillaumin Réunies.

Delio, Ilia. 1998. *Crucified love: Bonaventure's mysticism of the crucified Christ.* Quincy, IL: Franciscan Press.

Desoille, Robert. 1966. *The directed daydream.* Trans. Frank Haronian. New York: Psychosynthesis Research Foundation.

Despres, Denise. 1989. *Ghostly sights: Visual meditation in late-medieval literature.* Norman, OK: Pilgrim Books.

Devereux, George. 1958. Cultural thought models in primitive and modern psychiatric theories. *Psychiatry* 21:359–374.

Dinzelbacher, Peter. 1981. *Vision und visionsliterature im Mittelalter.* Monographien zür Geschichte des Mittelalters 23. Stuttgart: Anton Hiersemann.

du Moustier, Benoit. 1959. "Doctor discretus": Walter Hilton. *Cross and Crown* 11:292–300.

Dumont, Charles. 1999. *Praying the word of God: The use of* Lectio Divina. Oxford: SLG Press.

Eliade, Mircea. 1958. *Rites and symbols of initiation: The mysteries of birth and rebirth.* [Originally titled: "Birth and Rebirth."] Trans. Willard R. Trask. Repr. New York: Harper Colophon, 1975.

Emavardhana, Tipawadee, and Christopher D. Tori. 1997. Chnages in self-concept, ego defense mechanisms, and religiosity following seven-day vipassana meditation. *Journal for the Scientific Study of Religion* 36/2: 194–206.

Erickson, Carolly. 1976. *The medieval vision: Essays in history and perception.* New York: Oxford University Press.

Evagrius Ponticus. 1981. *The Praktikos. Chapters on prayer.* Trans. John Eudes Bamberger. Kalamazoo, MI: Cistercian Publications.

Fairbairn, W. R. D. 1952. *Psychoanalytic Studies of the Personality.* London: Routledge & Kegan Paul.

———. 1963. Synopsis of an object-relations theory of the personality. *International Journal of Psycho-Analysis* 44:224–25.

Fenichel, Otto. 1940. Psychoanalysis of anti-Semitism. *American Imago* 1:24–39.

———. 1945. *The psychoanalytic theory of neurosis.* New York: W. W. Norton.

Finamore, John. 1985. *Iamblichus and the theory of the vehicle of the soul.* Chico, CA: Scholars Press.

Finn, Mark. 1998. Tibetan Buddhism and comparative psychoanalysis. In *The couch and the tree: Dialogues in psychoanalysis and Buddhism,* ed., Anthony Molino, 161–69. New York: North Point Press.

———. 2003. Tibetan Buddhism and a mystical psychoanalysis. In *Psychoanalysis and Buddhism: An unfolding dialogue,* ed. Jeremy D. Safran, 101–15. Boston: Wisdom Publications.

Fishbane, Michael. 1994. *The kiss of God: Spiritual and mystical death in Judaism.* Seattle, WA: University of Washington Press.

Fleming, John V. 1977. *An introduction to the Franciscan literature of the Middle Ages.* Chicago: Franciscan Herald Press.

Flete, William. 1968. "Remedies against temptations": The third English version of William Flete. Eds. Edmund Colledge and Noel Chadwick. *Archivio Italiano per la Storia della Pietà* 5:201–240.

Flugel, J. C. 1945. *Man, morals and society: A psycho-analytical study.* Repr. New York: International Universities Press, 1970.

Fonagy, Peter, György Gergely, Elliot L. Jurist, and Mary Target. 2002. *Affect regulation, mentalization, and the development of the self.* New York: Other Press.

Forman, Robert K. C. 1990. Eckhart, *Gezücken,* and the ground of the soul. In *The problem of pure consciousness: Mysticism and philosophy,* ed. Robert K. C. Forman, 98–120. New York & Oxford: Oxford University Press.

Forster, Sophia E., and Donald L. Carveth. 1999. Christianity: A Kleinian perspective. *Canadian Journal of Psychoanalysis* 7:187–219.

Foxe, Arthur N. 1942. A psychomotor sequence (abreaction and catharsis). *Psychoanalytic Review* 29:127–30.

Freud, Sigmund. All references are to *The Standard Edition of the Complete Psychological Works of Sigmund Freud,* 24 vols., ed. James Strachey. London: Hogarth Press.

———. 1894. The neuro-psychoses of defence. *Standard Edition,* 3:45–61. London: Hogarth Press, 1962.

———. 1900. The interpretation of dreams. *Standard Edition,* 4–5:1–625. London: Hogarth Press, 1958.

———. 1910. Five lectures on psycho-analysis. *Standard Edition,* 11:9–55. London: Hogarth Press, 1957.

———. 1913. Totem and taboo: Some points of agreement between the mental life of savages and neurotics. *Standard Edition,* 13:1–161. London: Hogarth Press, 1958.

———. 1914a. On narcissism: An introduction. *Standard Edition,* 14:78–102. London: Hogarth Press, 1957.

———. 1921. Group psychology and the analysis of the ego. *Standard Edition,* 18:69–143. London: Hogarth Press, 1955.

———. 1926. Inhibitions, symptoms, and anxiety. *Standard Edition,* 20:87–172. London: Hogarth Press, 1959.

———. 1930. Civilization and its discontents. *Standard Edition,* 21:64–145. London: Hogarth Press, 1961.

———. 1933. New introductory lectures on psycho-analysis. *Standard Edition,* 22:5–182. London: Hogarth Press, 1964.

———. 1937. Analysis terminable and interminable. *Standard Edition*, 23:216–53. London: Hogarth Press, 1964.

Freud, Sigmund, and Oskar Pfister. 1963. *Psychoanalysis and faith: The letters of Sigmund Freud and Oskar Pfister*, ed. Heinrich Meng and Ernst L. Freud. New York: Basic Books.

Fromm, Erich. 1947. *Man for himself: An inquiry into the psychology of ethics.* New York: Holt, Rinehart & Winston. Repr. Greenwich, CT: Fawcett Publications, n.d.

Fry, Timothy, ed. 1982. *The rule of St. Benedict in English.* Collegeville, MN: Liturgical Press.

Gardner, Helen L. 1933. Walter Hilton and the authorship of the *Cloud of Unknowing. Review of English Studies* 19 (34): 129–47.

———. 1936a. The text of *The Scale of Perfection. Medium Aevum* 5 (1): 11–30.

———. 1936b. Walter Hilton and the mystical tradition in England. *Essays and Studies* 22:103–27.

Gardiner, Eileen. 1989. *Visions of heaven and hell before Dante.* New York: Italica Press.

Gertrude of Helfta. 1993. *The herald of divine love.* Trans. Margaret Winkworth. New York: Paulist Press.

Gill, Merton M. 1982. *Analysis of Transference.* Vol. 1. *Theory and technique.* New York: International Universities Press.

Gilson, Etienne. 1960. *The Christian philosophy of Saint Augustine.* Trans. L. E. M. Lynch. New York: Random House.

Glasscoe, Marion. 1993. *English medieval mystics: Games of faith.* London & New York: Longman.

Greenson, Ralph R. 1967. *The Technique and practice of psychoanalysis.* Vol. 1. New York: International Universities Press.

Gregory the Great, Saint. 1959. *Dialogues.* Trans. Odo John Zimmerman. Washington, DC: Catholic University of America Press.

Grossman, Lee. 1993. The significance of religious themes and fantasies during psychoanalysis. *Journal of the American Psychoanalytic Association* 41 (3): 755–64.

Guigo II. 1978. *The ladder of monks: A letter on contemplative life* and *twelve meditations.* Trans. Edmund Colledge and James Walsh. Garden City, NY: Doubleday.

Haartman, Keith. 2001. On "unitive distortions": Toward a differential assessment of religious ecstasy. *Psychoanalytic Review* 88 (6): 811–36.

———. 2004. *Watching and praying: personality transformation in eighteenth century British methodism.* Amsterdam: Editions Rodopi.

Hadot, Pierre. 2002. *What is ancient philosophy?* Trans. Michael Chase. Cambridge, MA & London, UK: Belknap Press of Harvard University Press.

Hall, Thelma. 1988. *Too deep for words: Rediscovering lectio divina.* New York: Paulist Press.

Hamburger, Jeffrey. 1989. The visual and the visionary: The image in late medieval monastic devotions. *Viator* 20:161–82.

Hanson, John S. 1980. Dreams and visions in the Graeco-Roman world and early Christianity. In *Aufstieg und Niedergang der Römischen Welt: Geschichte und Kultur Roms in Spiegel der Neuren Forschung.* Vol. 2.23.2. *Principat,* eds. Hildegard Temporini and Wolfgang Haase, 1395–427. Berlin: Walter de Gruyter.

Hartmann, Heinz. 1960. *Psychoanalysis and moral values.* New York: International Universities Press.

Hartmann, Heinz, and Rudolph M. Loewenstein. 1962. Notes on the superego. *Psychoanalytic Study of the Child* 17:42–81. Reprinted in *Papers on Psychoanalytic Psychology,* Heinz Hartmann, Ernst Kris, and Rudolph M. Loewenstein, 144–81. (Psychological Issues, Vol. 4, No. 2, Monograph 14). New York: International Universities Press, 1964.

Harvey, E. Ruth. 1975. *The inward wits: Psychological theory in the Middle Ages and the Renaissance.* London: Warburg Institute-University of London.

Hayes, Zachary. 1999. *Bonaventure: Mystical writings.* New York: Crossroad Publishing.

Hazzaya, Joseph. 1934. Mystical treatise. *Woodbrooke Studies* 7:177–84.

Hedrick, Charles W. 1981. Paul's conversion/call: A comparative analysis of the three reports in Acts. *Journal of Biblical Literature* 100:415–32.

Hilton, Walter. 1929. *Minor works of Walter Hilton.* Ed. Dorothy Jones. London: Burns Oates and Washbourne.

———. 1948. *The scale of perfection.* Ed. Evelyn Underhill. London: John M. Watkins.

———. 1952. *The goad of love: An unpublished translation of the* Stimulus Amoris *formerly attributed to St. Bonaventura.* Ed. Clare Kirchberger. London: Faber & Faber. Repr. New York: Harper and Brothers, n.d.

———. 1979. *The stairway of perfection.* Trans. M. L. Del Mastro. Garden City, NY: Image Books/Doubleday.

———. 1983. *Eight chapters on perfection* and *Angels' song.* Trans. Rosemary Dorward. Oxford: SLG Press.

———. 1991. *The scale of perfection.* Trans. John P. H. Clark and Rosemary Dorward. New York: Paulist Press.

Hodgson, Marshall G. S. 1974. *The venture of Islam: Conscience and history in a world civilization.* Vol. 2. *The expansion of Islam in the middle periods.* Chicago: University of Chicago Press.

Hopkins, Brooke. 1989. Jesus and object-use: A Winnicottian account of the resurrection myth. *International Review of Psycho-Analysis* 16:93–100.

Hugh of Saint-Victor. 1962. *Selected spiritual writings.* Trans. A Religious of C.S.M.V. London: Faber & Faber.

Hussey, S. S. 1980. Walter Hilton: Traditionalist? In *The medieval mystical tradition in England: Papers,* ed., Marion Glasscoe, 1–16. Papers read at rhe Exeter Symposium, July. Exeter, UK: University of Exeter.

Ignatius Loyola, St. 1963. *The spiritual exercises.* Trans. Thomas Corbishley. Repr. Wheathampstead: Anthony Clarke, 1973.

———. 1991. The spiritual exercises and *Selected works.* Ed. George E. Ganss, with Parmananda R. Divarkar, Edward Malatesta, and Martin E. Palmer. New York: Paulist Press.

Innes-Parker, Catherine. 1999. *Mi bodi hege with thi bodi neiled o rode*: The gendering of the Pauline concept of crucifixion with Christ in medieval devotional prose for women. *Studies in Religion/Sciences Religieuses* 28 (1): 49–61.

Isaac of Nineveh. 1923. *Mystical treatises by Isaac of Nineveh: Translated from Bedjan's Syriac Text with an Introduction and Registers.* Trans. A. J. Wensinck. Verhandelingen der Koninklijke Akademie van Wetenschappen te Amsterdam Afdeeling Letterkunde, Nieuwe Reeks, Deel XXII No. 1.) Amsterdam: Koninklijke Akademie van Wetenschappen.

Jacobson, Edith. 1964. *The self and the object world.* Journal of the American Psychoanalytic Association Monograph Series, No. 2. New York: International Universities Press.

Jarman, J. O. H. 1959. The Welsh Myrddin poems. In *Arthurian literature in the middle ages: A collaborative history,* ed. Roger Sherman Loomis, 20–29. Oxford: Clarendon Press.

Jeauneau, Edouard. 1987. Le renouveau erigenien du XIIe siecle. *Eriugena Redivivus: Zür Wirkungsgeschichte seines Denkens im Mettelalter und im Übergang zür Neuzeit.* Ed. Werner Beierwaltes. Heidelberg: Carl Winter-Universitatsverlag, 1987, pp. 26–46.

Jonas, Hans. 1969. Myth and mysticism: A study of objectification and interiorization in religious thought. *Journal of Religion* 49:315–29.

Jones, Ernest. 1944. The psychology of religion. In *Psychoanalysis Today,* ed. Sandor Lorand, 315–25. New York: International Universities Press.

Julian of Norwich. 1978. *Showings.* Trans. Edmund Colledge and James Walsh. New York: Paulist Press.

Jung, Carl Gustav. 1952. Foreword. In *Lucifer and Prometheus,* R. J. Zwi Werblowsky, London: Routledge & Kegan Paul. Repr., *Psychology and Religion: West and East.* 2nd ed. Trans. R. F. C. Hull. *Collected Works.* Vol. 11. Princeton, NJ: Princeton University Press, 1959.

Kakar, Sudhir. 1985. Psychoanalysis and religious healing: Siblings or strangers? *Journal of the American Academy of Religion* 53 (3): 841–53.

Katraya, Dadisho. 1934. A treatise on solitude, trans. A. J. Wensinck. *Woodbrooke Studies* 7:70–143.

Kieckhefer, Richard. 1984. *Unquiet souls: Fourteenth-century saints and their religious milieu.* Chicago: University of Chicago Press.

Kienzle, Beverly Mayne. 1953. Introduction. In *The Letters of St. Bernard of Clairvaux,* trans. Bruno Scott James. London: Burns and Oates, 1953. Repr., Stroud, UK: Sutton Publishing, 1998.

Kirschner, Suzanne R. 1996. *The religious and romantic origins of psychoanalysis: individuation and integration in post-Freudian theory*. Cambridge: University Press.

Klein, John W. 1961. Was Mercutio Christopher Marlowe? *Drama* 60:36–39.

Klein, Melanie. 1935. A contribution to the psychogenesis of manic-depressive states. Repr., *Love, guilt and reparation and other works. 1921–1945*, Melanie Klein, 262–89. New York: Delacorte Press, 1975.

———. 1937. Love, guilt and reparation. Repr. in *Love, guilt and reparation*, 306–43.

———. 1940. Mourning and its relation to manic-depressive states. Repr. in *Love, Guilt and Reparation*, 244–69.

Knowles, David. 1961. *The English mystical tradition*. London: Burns and Oates.

———. 1975. The influence of pseudo-Dionysius on Western mysticism. In *Christian Spirituality: Essays in Honour of Gordon Rupp*, ed. Peter Brooks, 81–94. London: SCM Press.

Kohut, Heinz. 1966. Forms and transformations of narcissism. *Journal of the American Psychoanayltic Association* 14:243–72.

———. 1971. *The analysis of the self: A systematic approach to the psychoanalytic treatment of narcissistic personality disorders*. Madison, CT: International Universities Press.

———. 1977. The restoration of the self. New York: International Universities Press.

Krojanker, Rolj J. 1966. Leuner's symbolic drama. *American Journal of Clinical Hypnosis* 9 (1): 56–61.

Kubie, Lawrence S. 1943. The use of induced hypnagogic reveries in the recovery of repressed amnesic data. *Bulletin of the Menninger Clinic* 7:172–82.

Langs, Robert J. 1978. A model of supervision: The patient as unconscious supervisor. In *Technique in Transition*, 587–625. New York: Jason Aronson.

———. 1994. *Doing supervision and being supervised*. London: Karnac Books.

Leuba, James H. 1925. *The psychology of religious mysticism*. Repr., London: Routledge & Kegan Paul, 1972.

Leuner, Hanscarl. 1969. Guided affective imagery (GAI): A method of intensive psychotherapy. *American Journal of Psychotherapy* 23 (1): 4–22.

———. 1975. The role of imagery in psychotherapy. In *New Dimensions in Psychiatry: A World View*, ed. Silvano Arieti and Gerard Chrzanowski, 169–99. New York: John Wiley & Sons.

———. 1977. Guided affective imagery: An account of its development. *Journal of Mental Imagery* 1 (1): 73–92.

———. 1978. Basic principles and therapeutic efficacy of guided affective imagery (GAI). Trans. Augusta Arthur. In *The power of human imagination: New methods in psychotherapy*, ed. Jerome L. Singer and Kenneth S. Pope, 125–66. New York: Plenum Press.

————. 1984. *Guided affective imagery: Mental imagery in short-term psychotherapy. The basic course.* Trans. Elizabeth Lachman. Ed. William A. Richards. New York: Thieme-Stratton, & Stuttgart: Georg Thieme Verlag.

Lifton, Robert Jay. 1956. "Thought reform" of Western civilians in Chinese communist prisons. *Psychiatry* 19:173–95.

————. 1961. *Thought reform and the psychology of totalism: A study of "brainwashing" in China.* New York: W. W. Norton.

Lindblom, Johannes. 1962. *Prophecy in ancient Israel.* Philadelphia: Fortress Press.

Loewald, Hans W. 1980. *Papers on psychoanalysis.* New Haven, CT: Yale University Press.

————. 1988. On the mode of therapeutic action of psychoanalytic psychotherapy. In *How does treatment help? On the modes of therapeutic action of psychoanalytic psychotherapy,* ed. Arnold Rothstein, 51–59. Madison, CT: International Universities Press.

Lohfink, Gerhard. 1976. *The conversion of St. Paul: Narrative and history in Acts.* Trans. Bruce J. Malina. Chicago: Franciscan Herald Press.

Lynn, Steven Jay, and Judith W. Rhue, eds. 1994. *Dissociation: Clinical and theoretical perspectives.* New York & London: Guilford Press.

Magrassi, Mariano. 1998. *Praying the Bible: An introduction to* Lectio Divina. Collegeville, MN: Liturgical Press.

Markus, Robert A. 1964. "Imago" and "similitudo" in Augustine. *Revue des Études Augustiniennes* 10:125–43.

Maslow, Abraham H. 1968. *Toward a psychology of being.* Repr. New York: D. Van Nostrand & Co., n.d.

McGinn, Bernard. 1976. Pseudo-Dionysius and the early Cistercians. In *One yet two: Monastic tradition east and west,* ed., M. Basil Pennington, 200–41. Kalamazoo, MI: Cistercian Publications.

————. 1991. *The foundations of mysticism: Origins to the fifth century.* Vol. 1. *The presence of God: A history of western Christian mysticism.* New York: Crossroad.

————. 1994. *The growth of mysticism: Gregory the Great through the 12th Century.* Vol. 2. *The presence of God: A history of western Christian mysticism.*) New York: Crossroad.

————. 1998. *The flowering of mysticism: Men and women in the new mysticism—1200–1350.* Vol. 3. *The presence of God: A history of western Christian mysticism.*) New York: Crossroad Herder.

McWilliams, Nancy. 1994. *Psychoanalytic diagnosis: Understanding personality structure in the clinical process.* New York & London: Guilford Press.

Mechthild of Magdeburg. 1953. *The revelations of Mechthild of Magdeburg (1210–1297). or, The flowing light of the godhead.* Trans. Lucy Menzies. London: Longmans, Green.

Meissner, W. W. 1999. *To the greater glory—A psychological study of Ignatian spirituality.* Milwaukee, WI: Marquette University Press.

Merkur, Dan. 1984. The nature of the hypnotic state: A psychoanalytic approach. *International Review of Psycho-Analysis* 11 (3): 345–354.

———. 1992a. *Becoming half hidden: Shamanism and initiation among the Inuit.* 2nd ed. New York: Garland Publications.

———. 1993. Mythology into metapsychology: Freud's misappropriation of Romanticism. *Psychoanalytic Study of Society* 18:345–60. Ed. L. Bryce Boyer, Ruth M. Boyer, and Stephen M. Sonnenberg. Hillsdale, NJ: Analytic Press.

———. 1995–96. "And he trusted in Yahweh": The transformation of Abram in Gen 12–13 and 15. *Journal of Psychology of Religion* 4–5:65–88.

———. 1998a. *The ecstatic imagination: Psychedelic experiences and the psychoanalysis of self-actualization.* Albany: State University of New York Press.

———. 1998b. The exemplary life. In *What is Religion? Origins, Definitions and Explanations,* ed. Thomas A. Idinopulos & Brian C. Wilson, 73–90. Leiden: E. J. Brill.

———. 1999. *Mystical moments and unitive thinking.* Albany: State University of New York Press.

———. 2000. *The mystery of manna: The psychedelic sacrament of the Bible.* Rochester, VT: Park Street Press.

———. 2001a. *The psychedelic sacrament: Manna, meditation, and mystical experience.* Rochester, VT: Park Street Press.

———. 2001b. *Unconscious wisdom: A Superego function in dreams, conscience, and inspiration.* Albany: State University of New York Press.

———. 2002. Spiritual alchemy in *King Lear. Theosophical History* 8 (10): 74–89.

———. 2004. Psychotherapeutic change in the Book of Job. In *Psychology and the Bible: A New Way to Read the Scriptures.* Vol. 2. *From Genesis to Apocalyptic Vision,* ed. J. Harold Ellens and Wayne G. Rollins, 119–39. New York: Greenwood-Praeger Publishers.

———. 2005. *Psychoanalytic approaches to myth: Freud and the Freudians.* New York & London: Routledge.

Merlan, Philip. 1963. *Monopsychism mysticism metaconsciousness: Problems of the soul in the neoaristotelian and neoplatonic tradition.* The Hague: Martinus Nijhoff.

Meyer, Jon. 1975. *Death and neurosis.* New York: International Universities Press.

Meyerson, Bernard G., and Louis Stollar. 1962. A psychoanalytical interpretation of the crucifixion. *Psychoanalysis and the Psychoanalytic Review* 49 (4): 117–118.

Milosh, Joseph E. 1966. *The scale of perfection and the English mystical tradition.* Madison, Milwaukee & London: University of Wisconsin Press.

Money-Kyrle, Roger E. 1944. Towards a common aim: A psychoanalytical contribution to ethics. *British Journal of Medical Psychology* 20. Repr. in *The collected papers of Roger Money-Kyrle,* ed. Donald Meltzer with Edna O'Shaughnessy, 176–97. Strath Tay, UK: Clunie Press.

Monk of Farne. 1961. *The meditations of a fourteenth century monk.* Ed. Dom Hugh Farmer. Baltimore: Helicon Press.

Morray-Jones, C. R. A. 1993a. Paradise revisited (2 Cor 12:1–12): The Jewish mystical background of Paul's apostolate. Part 1: The Jewish sources. *Harvard Theological Review* 86/2:177–217.

———. 1993b. Paradise revisited (2 Cor 12:1–12): The Jewish mystical background of Paul's apostolate. Part 2: Paul's heavenly ascent and its significance. *Harvard Theological Review* 86 (3): 265–92.

Mueller, Janel. 1991. Preface. In *The scale of perfection*, Walter Hilton, trans. John P. H. Clark and Rosemary Dorward, 1–11. New York & Mahwah, NJ: Paulist Press.

Newman, John W. 1996. *Disciplines of attention: Buddhist insight meditation, the ignatian spiritual exercises, and classical psychoanalysis.* New York & Bern: Peter Lang.

Nolan, Barbara. 1977. *The gothic visionary perspective.* Princeton, NJ: Princeton University Press.

Noye, Irénée, Charles Kannengiesser, Paul Agaesse, Jacques Hourlier, André Rayez, and Tomas de la Cruz. 1974. *Jesus in Christian devotion and contemplation,* trans. Paul J. Oligny. St. Meinrad, IN: Abbey Press.

Nygren, Anders. 1953. *Agape and eros.* Trans. Philip S. Watson. London: Society for Promoting Christian Knowledge.

Oakland, James A. 1974. Self-actualization and sanctification. *Journal of Psychology and Theology* 2/3: 202–9.

Ostow, Mortimer. 1996. *Myth and madness: The psychodynamics of antisemitism.* New Brunswick, NJ & London, UK: Transaction Publishers.

Owen, H. P. 1971. Christian mysticism: A study of Walter Hilton's *The ladder of perfection. Religious Studies* 7:31–42.

Patch, Howard Rollin. 1950. *The other world: According to descriptions in medieval literature.* Cambridge, MA: Harvard University Press. Repr., New York: Octagon Books, 1970.

Pennington, M. Basil. 1998. *Lectio Divina: Renewing the ancient practice of praying the scriptures.* New York: Crossroad Publishing.

Pepler, Conrad. 1958. *The English religious heritage.* London: Blackfriars Publications.

Petroff, E. A. 1986. *Medieval women's visionary literature.* London: Oxford University Press.

Pfister, Oskar. 1932. Instinctive psychoanalysis among the Navahos. *Journal of Nervous and Mental Disease* 76:234–54.

———. 1948. *Christianity and fear: A study in history and in the psychology and hygiene of religion.* Trans. W. H. Johnston. London: George Allen & Unwin.

Pivnicki, D. 1969. The beginnings of psychotherapy. *Journal of the History of the Behavioral Sciences* 5:238–47.

Pollard, William F. 1987. Mystical elements in a fifteenth-century prayer sequence: "The Festis and the Passion of Oure Lord Ihesu Crist." In *The medieval mystical tradition in England: Exeter symposium V. Papers read at Dartington Hall, July 1987,* ed. Marion Glasscoe 47–61. Cambridge: D. S. Brewer.

Porete, Marguerite. 1993. *The Mirror of simple souls.* Trans. Ellen L. Babinsky. New York & Mahwah, NJ: Paulist Press.

Porter, Joseph A. 1988. *Shakespeare's Mercutio: His history and drama.* Chapel Hill & London: University of North Carolina Press.

Proclus Diadochus. 1954. *Commentary on the first alcibiades of Plato.* Critical Text and Indexes by L. G. Westerinck. Amsterdam: North-Holland Publishing Co.

Pruyser, Paul W. 1976. *A dynamic psychology of religion.* New York: Harper & Row.

Pseudo-Dionysius the Areopagite. 1987. *The Complete Works.* Trans. Colm Luibheid. New York & Mahwah: Paulist Press.

Ragusa, Isa, trans. 1961. *Meditations on the life of Christ: An illustrated manuscript of the fourteenth century.* Ed. Isa Ragusa and Rosalie B. Green. Princeton, NJ: Princeton University Press.

Rahner, Karl. 1979. The doctrine of the "spiritual senses" in the Middle Ages. In *Theological Investigations.* Vol. 16. *Experience of the spirit: Source of theology,* 104–34. Trans. David Morland. New York: Seabury Press.

Reddy, Satish. 2001. Psychoanalytic reflections on the sacred Hindu text, the *Bhagavad Gita.* In *Does God help? Developmental and clinical aspects of religious belief,* ed. Salman Akhtar and Henri Parens, 153–75. Northvale, NJ: Aronson, 2001.

Reyher, Joseph. 1977. Spontaneous imagery: Implications for psychoanalysis, psychopathology, and psychotherapy. *Journal of Mental Imagery* 1 (2): 253–74.

———. 1978. Emergent uncovering psychotherapy: The use of imagoic and linguistic vehicles in objectifying psychodynamic processes. In *The power of human imagination: New methods in psychotherapy,* ed. Jerome L. Singer and Kenneth S. Pope, 51–93. New York: Plenum Press.

[Rich, Edmund.] 1905. *The Mirror of St. Edmund.* Trans. Francesca M. Steele. London: Burnes and Oates.

Richard of St. Victor. 1979. *The twelve patriarchs. The mystical ark. Book three of the trinity.* Trans. Grover A. Zinn. New York: Paulist Press.

Roberts, Julian, Andrew G. Watson, eds. 1990. *John Dee's library catalogue.* London: The Bibliographical Society.

Rolle, Richard. 1988. *The English writings.* Trans. and ed., Rosamund Allen. New York & Mahwah, NJ: Paulist Press.

Runciman, Steven. 1968. *A history of the crusades,* Vol. 2. Harmondsworth: Penguin Books.

Russell-Smith, Joy. 1959. Walter Hilton. *The Month* 22:133–148.

Sacks, Howard L. 1979. The effect of spiritual exercises on the integration of self-system. *Journal of the Scientific Study of Religion* 18 (1): 46–50.

Salter, Elizabeth. 1974. *Nicholas Love's "Myrrour of the blessed lyf of Jesu Christ.* Analecta Cartusiana 10. Salzburg: Institut für Englische Sprache und Literatur.

Sandler, Joseph, and Bernard Rosenblatt. 1962. The concept of the representational world. *Psychoanalytic Study of the Child* 17:128–45.

Savage, Anne, and Nicholas Watson, trans. 1991. *Anchoritic spirituality:* Ancrene Wisse *and associated works.* New York & Mahwah: Paulist Press.

Schwartz, Lester. 1971. Superego analysis. Charles Brenner's section of the Ernst Kris study group. *Psychoanalytic Quarterly* 40:189–90.

Scupoli, Dom Lorenzo. 1945. *The spiritual combat:* and *A treatise on peace of soul.* Trans. William Lester and Robert Mohan. Westminster, MD: Newman Bookshop. Repr., Rockford, IL: TAN Books and Publishers.

Segal, Alan F. 1980. Heavenly ascent in Hellenistic Judaism, early Christianity, and their environment. *Augstieg under Niedergang der Römischen Welt, Principat II,* 23:1333–94. Ed. Wolfgang Haase. Berlin: Walter de Gruyter.

———. 1990. *Paul the convert: The apostolate and apostasy of Saul the Pharisee.* New Haven: Yale University Press.

Shor, Ronald E. 1959. Hypnosis and the concept of the generalized reality orientation. *American Journal of Psychotherapy* 13:582–602.

Showalter, Elaine. 1997. *Hystories: Hysterical epidemics and modern media.* New York: Columbia University Press.

Silber, Austin. 1989. Panic attacks facilitating recall and mastery: Implications for psychoanalytic technique. *Journal of the American Psychoanalytic Association* 37:337–64.

Silverman, Lloyd H. 1987. Imagery as an aid in working through unconscious conflicts: A preliminary report. *Psychoanalytic Psychology* 4 (1): 45–64.

Simmel, Ernst. 1946. Anti-Semitism and mass psychopathology. In *Anti-Semitism: A social disease,* 33–78. New York: International Universities Press.

Sitwell, Gerard. 1949–50. Contemplation in *"The scale of perfection." Downside Review* 67:276–90; 68:21–34, 271–89.

———. 1953. Introduction. In *The scale of perfection,* ed. Walter Hilton, trans. Gerard Sitwell, v–xviii. London: Burns and Oates.

Socarides, Charles W. 1978. *Homosexuality.* New York & London: Jason Aronson.

Stanley, David M. 1953. Paul's conversion in Acts: Why the three accounts? *Catholic Biblical Quarterly* 15:315–38.

Stephen of Sawley. 1984. *Treatises.* Trans. Jeremiah F. O'Sullivan. Ed. Bede K. Lackner. Kalamazoo, MI: Cistercian Publications.

Sterba, Richard. 1968. Remarks on mystic states. *American Imago* 25:77–85.

Stone, Leo. 1961. *The psychoanalytic situation: An examination of its development and essential nature.* New York: International Universities Press.

Suso, Henry. 1989. *The exemplar, with two German sermons*. New York: Paulist Press.

Suttie, Ian D. 1935. *The origins of love and hate*. London: Kegan Paul, Trench, Trubner. Repr., London: Free Association Books, 1988.

Symington, Neville. 1993. *Narcissism: A new theory*. London: Karnac Books.

———. 1994. *Emotion and spirit: Questioning the claims of psychoanalysis and religion.* London: Cassell; reprinted London: Karnac Books, 1998.

———. 2004. *The blind man sees: Freud's awakening and other essays*. London & New York: Karnac.

Tabor, James D. 1986. *Things unutterable: Paul's ascent to paradise in its Greco-Roman, Judaic, and early Christian contexts*. Lanham, MD: University Press of America.

Tarachow, Sidney. 1960. Judas, the beloved executioner. *Psychoanalytic Quarterly* 29:528–54.

Teresa of Jesus [of Avila]. 1946. *Complete works*. 3 vols. Trans. E. Allison Peers. London: Sheed & Ward.

Tobin, Frank. 1995. Medieval thought on visions and its resonance in Mechthild von Magdeburg's *Flowing light of the Godhead*. In *Vox Mystica: essays on medieval mysticism in honor of Professor Valerie M. Lagorio*, ed., Anne Clark Bartlett, with Thomas H. Bestul, Janet Goebel, and William F. Pollard, 41–53. Cambridge, UK: D. S. Brewer.

Ugolino di Monte Santa Maria. 1958. *The little flowers of St. Francis*. Trans. Raphael Brown. Garden City, NY: Image/Doubleday.

Underhill, Evelyn. 1933. *Mixed pasture: Twelve essays and addresses*. London: Methuen.

———. 1948. Introduction. In Walter Hilton, *The scale of perfection*, ed. Evelyn Underhill, v–lii. London: John M. Watkins.

van den Berg, J. H. 1962. An existential explanation of the guided daydream in psychotherapy. *Review of Existential Psychology and Psychiatry* 2:5–35.

Wakelin, M. F. 1980. English mysticism and the English homiletic tradition. In *The medieval mystical tradition in England*, ed., Marion Glasscoe, 39–54. Papers read at The Exeter Symposium. Exeter, UK: University of Exeter.

Ward, Benedicta, trans. 1975. *The sayings of the desert fathers: The alphabetical collection*. Kalamazoo, MI: Cistercian Publications, & Oxford: A. R. Mowbray.

Warren, Anne K. 1985. *Anchorites and their patrons in medieval England*. Berkeley: University of California Press.

White, Victor. 1944. *Walter Hilton: An English spiritual guide*. Guild Lecture No. 31. London: Guild of Pastoral Psychology.

Whitmont, Edward C. 1969. *The symbolic quest: Basic concepts of analytical psychology*. New York: G. P. Putnam's Sons. Repr., Princeton: Princeton University Press, 1978.

Widengren, Geo. 1961. Researches in Syrian mysticism: Mystical experiences and spiritual exercises. *Numen* 8 (3): 161–198.

William of St. Thierry. 1954. *The meditations of William of St. Thierry: Meditativae orationes*. Trans. a Religious of C.S.M.V. London: A. R. Mowbray.

—. 1969. *Exposition on the song of songs*. Trans. Columba Hart. Kalamazoo, MI: Cistercian Publications.

—. 1970. *On contemplating God. Prayer. Meditations*. Trans. Sister Penelope, C.S.M.V. Kalamazoo, MI: Cistercian Publications.

Winnicott, D. W. 1935. The manic defence. In *Through paediatrics to psycho-analysis: collected papers*, 129–44. New York: Basic Books, 1975. Repr., New York: Brunner/Mazel, Publishers.

—. 1948. Reparation in respect of mother's organized defence against depression. In *Through paediatrics to psycho-analysis*, 91–96.

—. 1950–55. Aggression in relation to emotional development. In *Through paediatrics to psycho-analysis*, 204–218.

—. 1952. Psychoses and child care. In *Through paediatrics to psycho-analysis*, 219–28.

—. 1954–55. The depressive position in normal emotional development. In *Through paediatrics to psycho-analysis*, 262–77.

—. 1960. The theory of the parent-infant relationship. *International Journal of Psycho-Analysis* 41:585–95. Repr. in *The maturational processes and the facilitating environment: studies in the theory of emotional development*, 37–55. New York: International Universities Press.

—. 1963a. The development of the capacity for concern. *Bulletin of the Menninger Clinic* 27:167–76. Repr. in *The maturational processes and the facilitating environment*, 73–82.

—. 1963b. Communicating and not communicating leading to a study of certain opposites. Repr. in *The maturational processes and the facilitating environment*, 179–92.

—. 1969. The use of an object and relating through identifications. *International Journal of Psycho-Analysis* 50. Repr. in *Playing and reality*. London: Tavistock Publications, 1971. Repr., Harmondsworth: Penguin Books, 1974, 101–11.

—. 1971. *Playing and reality*. London: Tavistock Publications. Repr., Harmondsworth: Penguin Books, 1974.

—. 1989. Fear of breakdown. In *psycho-analytic exploration*, ed. Clare Winnicott, Ray Shepherd, and Madeleine Davis, 87–95. London: Karnac Books.

Wolfson, Harry Austryn. 1935. The internal senses in Latin, Arabic, and Hebrew philosophic texts. *Harvard Theological Review* 28 (2): 69–133.

Wolters, Clifton, trans. 1961. *The cloud of unknowing*. Harmondsworth: Penguin Books.

Yates, Frances A. 1964. *Giordano Bruno and the hermetic tradition*. London: Routledge & Kegan Paul; Chicago: University of Chicago Press.

Zaleski, Carol. 1987. *Otherworld journeys: Accounts of near-death experience in medieval and modern times*. New York: Oxford University Press.

Zilboorg, Gregory. 1943. Fear of death. *Psychoanalytic Quarterly* 12:465–75.

Zilboorg, Gregory, with George W. Henry. 1941. *A history of medical psychology*. New York: W. W. Norton.

Zinn, Jr., Grover A. 1973. Mandala symbolism and use in the mysticism of Hugh of St. Victor. *History of Religions* 12:317–41.

Index